# Echoes of the Past: America's Fascist Parallels

Pete Cossaboon

ISBN: **9798300809478**

To the countless opportunities for growth and empowerment that have come my way, disguised as challenges and obstacles, I extend my deepest gratitude. It is through these experiences that I have come to understand my own innate divinity and the power that lies within each of us.

I envision a world where every individual recognizes their own divine nature, stepping into their personal power and manifesting a life filled with purpose, love, and abundance. May this book serve as a catalyst for that transformation, inspiring each reader to embrace their true self and create a life beyond their wildest dreams.

Together, let us embark on this journey of self-discovery, empowerment, and spiritual growth, co-creating a world that is a reflection of our highest potential and deepest desires.

Love.  Peace.  Release.

# Introduction: The Specter of Fascism

- Overview of rising authoritarian tendencies in the U.S.
- Importance of recognizing historical patterns.
- Goal: Equip readers with tools to analyze and resist modern parallels.

---

# Part I: Foundations of Fascism

## 1. The Anatomy of Fascism

- Defining fascism through history: Italy, Germany, and beyond.
- Key characteristics: authoritarianism, ultranationalism, and propaganda.

## 2. The Mythic Past

- Role of nostalgia in fascist rhetoric: idealized histories and patriarchal norms.
- Historical use of myth to justify exclusion and hierarchy.

## 3. The Rise of Fascist Movements

- Economic and social conditions fueling fascism in 20th-century Europe.
- Lessons from the Great Depression and post-WWI Germany.

## 4. Early American Flirtations with Fascism

- Historical movements like the German-American Bund and America First.
- Figures like Charles Lindbergh and Father Coughlin.

---

# Part II: Modern Parallels

## 5. The Cult of Personality

- Charismatic leaders: building loyalty and suppressing dissent.
- Comparisons between historical and contemporary political figures.

## 6. Nationalism and Grievance Politics

- Exploiting economic and cultural grievances to build unity through division.
- Modern echoes in "America First" and similar rhetoric.

## 7. Undermining Democratic Institutions

- Historical examples: dismantling courts, elections, and checks on power.
- Current trends in questioning election integrity and judicial independence.

## 8. The Role of Propaganda

- From radio broadcasts to social media algorithms.
- The evolution of disinformation as a tool for control.

## 9. Creating Us vs. Them

- Dehumanizing minority groups: parallels in historical and contemporary rhetoric.
- The politics of exclusion and identity.

## 10. Law and Order as a Weapon

- Historical fascist use of "law and order" to suppress dissent.
- Contemporary parallels in criminal justice and immigration policies.

# Part III: Economic and Social Conditions

## 11. The Role of Economic Anxiety

- How economic insecurity fosters extremism.
- Historical and modern examples of leveraging economic fears.

## 12. Cultural Shifts and Backlash

- The role of gender, sexuality, and race in authoritarian rhetoric.
- Fascism's fixation on patriarchal and heteronormative structures.

## 13. The Erosion of Truth

- How fascist politics undermines truth through unreality and conspiracy theories.
- Parallels in the post-truth era.

## 14. Weaponizing Education and Intellectuals

- Historical suppression of intellectual freedom.
- Contemporary attacks on academia and critical thinking.

# Part IV: Resistance and Prevention

## 15. Lessons from the Anti-Fascist Struggle

- How movements resisted fascism historically.
- Case studies from WWII and modern antifascist actions.

## 16. The Role of Civic Engagement

- Building resilient communities through grassroots activism.
- Practical steps for citizen resistance to authoritarianism.

## 17. Strengthening Democratic Institutions

- Recommendations for protecting the judiciary, press, and elections.
- The role of checks and balances in preserving democracy.

## 18. Combating Propaganda and Disinformation

- Strategies for identifying and countering modern information warfare.
- Tools to rebuild trust in institutions.

## 19. Bridging Divides

- Reducing polarization to foster unity.
- Building coalitions across political and social divides.

---

# Conclusion: A Call to Vigilance

## 20. Safeguarding Democracy for the Future

- The importance of learning from history to recognize warning signs.
- Call to action: embracing collective responsibility to prevent the rise of authoritarianism.

# Foreword

When Barack Obama was elected President and marriage equality became the law of the land, I felt like America was finally beginning to accept the ideals of fairness and inclusion as deeply as I had learned to accept myself later in life. As someone who came out as gay in middle age, this period felt like a watershed moment, not only for the country but for me personally. It seemed as though the world was starting to value the diversity and humanity that I had come to embrace within myself. As the brother of a special-needs individual, I believed that his care, dignity, and place in society were becoming as significant to the world as they had always been to me.

But in the years that followed, that sense of progress began to unravel. With the rise of Christian nationalism, Donald Trump, and growing fascist movements across the West, a new narrative began to take shape—one that declared the only appropriate viewpoint belonged to straight, white, cisgender men, particularly those with wealth and power. Anyone who didn't fit that mold was required, implicitly or explicitly, to seek their permission to exist, participate, and thrive.

I began to see my own story—the tale of an individual striving for authenticity, equity, and inclusion—being erased from the larger narrative of America. While I am fully aware of the privilege I carry as a white, cisgender man, I also cannot sit idly by while I watch a nation, one that I believe was built on the rule of law, fairness, equality, diversity, and inclusion for all people, become transformed into an instrument of power that benefits only the already empowered. The result, as I see it, is a systematic stripping away of the rights, opportunities, and dignity of everyone else.

This book is my response. It is both a source of information and a call to action—not just for me, but for anyone who feels marginalized, overlooked, or unrepresented. It is also a message to my grandson, so he will know who his Pop Pop is, what I stood for, and the kind of world I fought to preserve for him.

In writing *Echoes of the Past: America's Fascist Parallels*, I hope to provide clarity about where we've been, how we arrived at this moment, and what we can do to resist the forces of oppression. This is not just a story about history repeating itself; it is a warning and a guidebook for ensuring the values of democracy, inclusion, and equality endure.

# What is Fascism?

Fascism is more than a political ideology; it is a method of control that seeks to reshape society through authoritarianism, ultranationalism, and the suppression of dissent. At its core, fascism thrives on division, creating a binary of "us" versus "them" to justify the concentration of power in the hands of a few. It is marked by the elevation of a single leader or ruling class as the sole arbiter of truth, morality, and the national identity, often at the expense of marginalized groups.

Historically, fascism manifests through several distinct characteristics:

- **Authoritarianism**: The subversion or outright dismantling of democratic institutions to centralize power.
- **Ultranationalism**: The promotion of a hyper-patriotic, often exclusionary identity tied to race, religion, or culture.
- **Suppression of Dissent**: The elimination of opposing viewpoints through censorship, propaganda, and violence.
- **Mythic Past**: An idealized vision of a bygone era used to stoke nostalgia and justify oppressive policies.
- **Propaganda and Disinformation**: The strategic manipulation of media to control narratives and foster mistrust of objective truths.
- **Economic and Social Hierarchies**: The enforcement of rigid societal roles, often reinforcing the dominance of straight, white, cisgender men and the marginalization of everyone else.

Fascism is not confined to a specific time or place. It can emerge in any society where fear, division, and inequality create fertile ground for its growth. It is adaptive, adopting the language and tools of the moment—whether it be 20th-century rallies or 21st-century social media—to advance its goals.

For the purposes of this book, fascism is defined not solely by its historical forms but by its enduring tactics and outcomes. Fascism is the pursuit of power by exploiting fear, rewriting history, and silencing dissent, all while upholding a rigid hierarchy that serves the privileged at the expense of the marginalized.

Understanding this definition is key to recognizing how fascist patterns manifest today. It equips us to identify and challenge these forces wherever they arise, ensuring that democracy and inclusion remain the pillars of our shared society.

## Introduction: The Specter of Fascism

In recent years, the political and social fabric of the United States has experienced a palpable shift. Rising authoritarian tendencies have emerged, from the erosion of democratic norms to the proliferation of divisive rhetoric that pits citizens against one another. This is not the hyperbole of a concerned few—it is a pattern scholars, activists, and ordinary citizens alike have begun to notice with growing alarm. These tendencies may not yet fully replicate the fascist regimes of the past, but the echoes are unmistakable and ominous.

Authoritarianism does not arrive overnight, nor does it announce itself with fanfare. It creeps in through small cracks: an undermining of trust in elections, the normalization of disinformation, and the amplification of fears that stoke division. In America today, we see the seeds of such developments in efforts to delegitimize the press, undermine judicial independence, and disenfranchise voters. The rise of militias emboldened by political leaders, the systematic marginalization of certain groups, and the strategic use of disinformation have combined to create a chilling atmosphere where the unthinkable begins to feel inevitable.

This book is not a proclamation of doom but a call to vigilance. To confront the specter of fascism, we must understand its origins, mechanisms, and the subtle ways it infiltrates democratic societies. History provides us with a roadmap. The fascist regimes of the 20th century—Nazi Germany, Mussolini's Italy, and Franco's Spain—were not aberrations that sprang up in a vacuum. They were built on existing grievances, economic instability, and a deliberate exploitation of societal divides. Recognizing these historical patterns is crucial if we are to resist their modern parallels.

The goal of this book is to provide readers with the tools to analyze the present through the lens of the past. It aims to identify the hallmarks of fascist movements—both subtle and overt—and to empower individuals to resist them effectively. Through a blend of historical analysis and contemporary examination, this book will uncover the strategies that authoritarian leaders use to consolidate power and suppress dissent.

Fascism thrives in apathy and ignorance. By the time its grip is fully felt, it is often too late to reverse course. That is why understanding these patterns now is essential. The United States, like all democracies, is not immune to the forces of authoritarianism. It is not invulnerable to leaders who prioritize personal power over the collective good or movements that seek to rewrite its founding ideals to serve a narrow few.

This is not just a story about history repeating itself—it is a warning and a guidebook for those who refuse to let history dictate the future. Together, we will explore the parallels between past and present, not as passive observers, but as active participants in shaping what comes next. The specter of fascism is not inevitable, but resisting it requires vigilance, courage, and a commitment to the values that make democracy worth defending. Let this be a step toward ensuring that those values endure.

## Part I: Foundations of Fascism

## Chapter 1: The Anatomy of Fascism

To understand the danger posed by modern authoritarian movements, it is essential to dissect the anatomy of fascism itself. Historically, fascism emerged as a response to periods of economic instability, cultural upheaval, and political fragmentation. It is not bound by geography or time—it is a method of control, a blueprint for consolidating power by exploiting division, fear, and grievances. By examining its historical roots in Italy, Germany, and other nations, we can uncover its defining characteristics and how they resurface in new forms today.

## Fascism in History: Italy and Germany

Fascism first took political shape in post-World War I Italy, under Benito Mussolini. Disillusioned by the failures of liberal democracy and rattled by the economic crises that followed the war, Italians turned to Mussolini's promise of national revival. Mussolini's movement emphasized **authoritarianism**, **ultranationalism**, and **propaganda**, all elements that would become hallmarks of fascist regimes.

In Germany, Adolf Hitler and the Nazi Party adapted Mussolini's playbook, amplifying its methods with the industrial efficiency and racial ideologies that defined the Third Reich. Germany in the 1930s, much like Italy, was reeling from economic instability and the perceived humiliation of the Treaty of Versailles. Hitler's ability to blend fascist principles with Germany's specific cultural grievances—such as antisemitism and the myth of Aryan superiority—demonstrated fascism's adaptability to local contexts.

Beyond these two infamous examples, fascist movements have taken root in Spain under Franco, Japan under its wartime imperial government, and in other nations where conditions allowed for the suppression of dissent and the elevation of a singular, authoritarian vision.

## The Defining Characteristics of Fascism

Across its many forms, fascism is identifiable by several core traits:

# 1. Authoritarianism

Fascism relies on the concentration of power in a single leader or ruling class, often bypassing or dismantling democratic institutions. Mussolini famously declared that fascism should better be called "corporatism" because it merges the power of the state with corporate interests. In practice, this meant suppressing dissent, banning opposition parties, and centralizing authority under a "supreme" figure.

In Germany, Hitler used the Reichstag Fire as a pretext to implement the **Enabling Act**, which effectively gave him dictatorial powers. The erosion of democratic norms under both Mussolini and Hitler demonstrates fascism's foundational reliance on authoritarianism as a means to consolidate power.

---

# 2. Ultranationalism

Fascism glorifies a singular national identity, often rooted in race, religion, or culture, and frames that identity as superior to all others. This hyper-patriotic fervor fuels exclusionary policies, targeting groups seen as "others" or threats to the purity of the nation.

In Mussolini's Italy, ultranationalism took the form of reviving the Roman Empire's grandeur, a nostalgic appeal to Italy's past as a justification for imperial ambitions. In Nazi Germany, ultranationalism was weaponized through racial purity laws and the ideology of Lebensraum, or "living space," which justified territorial expansion at the expense of others.

---

# 3. Propaganda

Propaganda is the lifeblood of fascist regimes, used to control narratives, shape public opinion, and create a unified vision of reality. Fascist propaganda relies heavily on emotional appeals—fear, pride, and hatred—rather than rational argument.

Both Mussolini and Hitler employed mass media to their advantage. Mussolini controlled Italy's press, ensuring his messaging dominated public discourse. Hitler, with the help of Joseph Goebbels, elevated propaganda to an art form, using newspapers, films, and massive rallies to create an image of unity and power that hid the regime's violent underpinnings.

The core strategy of propaganda is to create an **"us versus them" dichotomy**, where "us" represents the virtuous, patriotic majority and "them" are the scapegoats blamed for society's ills. This polarization is crucial for rallying support and suppressing dissent.

## A Playbook for Control

While the historical contexts of Italy and Germany differ, the methods of fascism share striking similarities. These regimes exploited fear—of economic collapse, cultural decline, and perceived enemies—while presenting a strong leader as the only solution. They silenced opposition through violence, undermined democratic institutions, and rewrote national narratives to align with their authoritarian goals.

Understanding these patterns allows us to see how fascism is not merely a historical phenomenon but a recurring method of control that adapts to the anxieties of any era. In the chapters to come, we will explore how these same characteristics manifest in modern times, offering a chilling reminder that the anatomy of fascism is as relevant now as it was a century ago.

By dissecting its anatomy, we arm ourselves with the knowledge to recognize it and the tools to resist its insidious rise.

## Chapter 2: The Mythic Past

Fascism thrives on the power of stories—especially stories about a past that never truly existed. By crafting an idealized version of history, fascist movements create a "mythic past," a vision of a time when society was pure, orderly, and thriving under traditional values. This past is depicted not as an era of nuance and complexity, but as a golden age whose supposed virtues were lost to progress, diversity, and liberalism. The mythic past is a cornerstone of fascist rhetoric, invoked to inspire nostalgia, justify exclusion, and reinforce rigid hierarchies.

## Nostalgia as a Political Weapon

Nostalgia is a potent force. It is a longing not just for what was, but for what people believe should have been. Fascist rhetoric exploits this emotional connection, presenting an idealized history where social order was clear, cultural identity was pure, and traditional hierarchies went unchallenged. In this imagined world, men were strong providers, women were dutiful mothers, and society was free from the "corrupting" influences of foreign ideas, diverse cultures, and changing norms.

In Mussolini's Italy, the myth of the Roman Empire's grandeur became the foundation of fascist propaganda. Mussolini portrayed himself as the modern Caesar, promising to restore Italy's greatness by uniting its people under one identity and pursuing imperial conquests. His rhetoric invoked the glory of Roman legions, ignoring the historical realities of Rome's diversity and complex governance in favor of a simplified narrative that suited his authoritarian ambitions.

Similarly, Adolf Hitler framed Nazi ideology around the myth of the Aryan race, claiming a lost golden age of racial purity and dominance. This narrative fueled policies of exclusion and violence, positioning Jews, Romani people, and other minorities as scapegoats for Germany's post-World War I hardships. Hitler's rhetoric offered a seductive promise: by eradicating these "threats," Germany could reclaim its rightful place in history.

## The Patriarchal Family as National Archetype

Central to the mythic past is the image of the patriarchal family, where the father rules as the ultimate authority, the mother nurtures, and children obey. Fascist movements elevate this family structure as the ideal model for society, using it to justify authoritarian control and social hierarchies. The leader of the fascist state is likened to the father of the nation—strong, protective, and deserving of unquestioning loyalty.

For example:

- Nazi propaganda glorified motherhood as the highest calling for women, portraying them as the guardians of racial purity and national strength. Women were celebrated for bearing children, not for their individuality or contributions outside the home.
- In Francoist Spain, the regime idealized a rural, Catholic past where families were strictly patriarchal, using this vision to suppress feminist movements and LGBTQ+ identities.

By tying the structure of the state to the patriarchal family, fascist regimes reinforce a hierarchy where men dominate and others—women, minorities, and dissenters—are subordinate. This vision deliberately ignores the diversity and complexity of real families and societies, substituting a rigid ideal that serves authoritarian goals.

---

**Myths as Justification for Exclusion and Hierarchy**

The mythic past is not just a nostalgic fantasy; it is a strategic tool for exclusion. By defining an ideal history, fascist movements create a clear distinction between those who belong and those who do not. Those who fit the ideal—typically straight, white, cisgender men in Western contexts—are positioned as the rightful heirs to the nation's legacy. Everyone else is cast as an intruder or a threat.

- **Cultural Purity:** Fascist myths often center on the idea of cultural contamination. In Nazi Germany, this took the form of antisemitism, with Jews depicted as corrupting forces undermining the Aryan ideal. Today, similar rhetoric targets immigrants, refugees, and religious minorities, portraying them as threats to national identity.
- **Racial Superiority:** Myths of racial purity, like those seen in Nazi Germany or apartheid South Africa, justify policies of segregation, disenfranchisement, and violence. By elevating one group as the custodians of a glorious past, fascist regimes marginalize others, erasing their contributions to history.
- **Traditional Gender Roles:** The mythic past reinforces rigid gender roles, portraying feminism, LGBTQ+ identities, and gender equity as modern corruptions. This narrative is used to justify policies that restrict reproductive rights, criminalize same-sex relationships, and suppress gender diversity.

---

## The Danger of the Mythic Past

The mythic past is dangerous precisely because it is seductive. It appeals to our desire for simplicity in complex times, offering the illusion of clarity and order. But this vision is not a reflection of history—it is a distortion, designed to erase inconvenient truths and empower those at the top of the hierarchy.

By understanding how fascist movements construct and weaponize the mythic past, we can begin to resist its allure. History is not a static story of glory or decline; it is a tapestry of struggles, achievements, and progress. Recognizing the falsehoods embedded in nostalgic rhetoric is essential to preserving the diversity, inclusion, and equality that are the true hallmarks of a just society.

In the next chapter, we will examine how these myths, combined with authoritarianism and ultranationalism, fuel the cult of personality that sustains fascist movements. By dissecting the mechanics of these tactics, we can arm ourselves against their corrosive influence in modern politics.

## Chapter 3: The Rise of Fascist Movements

Fascism does not emerge in a vacuum. It thrives in the fertile ground of economic instability, social fragmentation, and cultural upheaval. In the 20th century, the rise of fascist movements in Europe followed catastrophic periods of war and economic collapse. These conditions created a perfect storm: widespread disillusionment with existing systems, a desperate population seeking stability, and opportunistic leaders offering authoritarian solutions. By examining the roots of fascism in post-World War I Europe, we can uncover the forces that fueled its rise and draw lessons for today.

## Economic Conditions: The Cost of Crisis

### Post-WWI Instability

World War I left Europe in ruins—physically, economically, and politically. The Treaty of Versailles, signed in 1919, imposed severe reparations on Germany, plunging the country into financial despair. The German economy spiraled into hyperinflation, rendering money almost worthless. By 1923, everyday necessities like bread required wheelbarrows of cash, and savings were wiped out overnight. This economic chaos bred anger, humiliation, and a thirst for scapegoats.

Similarly, Italy emerged from the war with deep economic and social fractures. Despite being on the victorious side, Italy's economy suffered from high unemployment, strikes, and social unrest. Returning soldiers, promised a land of opportunity, found themselves in a country unable to deliver.

### The Great Depression

The stock market crash of 1929 reverberated across the globe, plunging Europe further into economic despair. In Germany, unemployment soared to 30%, and industrial output collapsed. The desperation of millions created fertile ground for radical ideologies. Fascists, particularly Adolf Hitler's Nazi Party, exploited this desperation by offering simple, direct solutions: restore national pride, punish the perceived culprits, and rebuild the economy through unity and discipline.

In Italy, Mussolini similarly capitalized on economic discontent. He promised economic stability through state intervention, public works programs, and the suppression of labor strikes. While these promises often went unfulfilled, they resonated with a population that saw no solutions from the fractured liberal government.

---

## Social Fragmentation: A World Divided

### Class Tensions

Economic instability magnified existing class divisions. In Germany, the working class became disillusioned with both capitalist elites and ineffective socialist movements. The Nazi Party presented itself as a "third way," uniting workers, farmers, and the middle class under the banner of nationalism.

In Italy, Mussolini portrayed himself as a mediator between the classes, promising to suppress the Bolshevik-inspired strikes that terrified industrialists while addressing the grievances of workers. By positioning fascism as a force for national unity, he exploited fears on both sides of the class divide.

### Cultural Anxiety

Fascist movements also exploited cultural anxieties. In the wake of WWI, Europe was grappling with rapid social changes: women entering the workforce, urbanization, and a perceived loss of traditional values. Fascist leaders framed these changes as threats to national identity, blaming them on liberalism, socialism, and minority groups.

In Germany, the Nazi Party targeted Jews, communists, and other minorities as scapegoats for societal decline. Hitler's rhetoric vilified them as corrupting forces undermining the "purity" of German culture. In Italy, Mussolini similarly blamed social unrest on foreign ideologies, portraying himself as a defender of Italian heritage.

---

## The Fascist Promise: Order from Chaos

Fascist leaders did not merely highlight grievances—they offered a vision of restoration and revival. This vision often included:

1. **Economic Stability**: Through public works, militarization, and suppression of dissent.
2. **National Unity**: By erasing political pluralism and marginalizing "undesirable" groups.
3. **Cultural Revival**: Through the glorification of a mythic past and the promise of national greatness.

Mussolini's Italy was framed as the heir to the Roman Empire, with fascism as the ideology that would restore Italy's rightful place in the world. Hitler offered Germans the idea of a "Thousand-Year Reich," a racial utopia that would dominate Europe and erase the humiliations of the Treaty of Versailles.

These promises were intoxicating to populations desperate for stability and purpose. The clarity and simplicity of fascist messaging contrasted sharply with the chaos of fragmented democratic systems, which often seemed unable to respond to crises decisively.

## Lessons for Today

The rise of fascism in 20th-century Europe offers critical lessons about the conditions that allow authoritarian movements to flourish:

1. **Economic Despair Breeds Extremism**: Economic instability creates a vulnerable population willing to embrace radical solutions. Modern parallels can be seen in the global economic fallout from the 2008 financial

crisis and the COVID-19 pandemic.

2. **Scapegoating as a Tool of Power**: Fascist leaders unify their base by identifying "enemies" within the population. Today, similar tactics are employed to demonize immigrants, religious minorities, and political opponents.

3. **The Erosion of Trust in Institutions**: In Italy and Germany, liberal governments were seen as weak, corrupt, and unable to address crises. In the modern era, declining trust in democratic institutions similarly paves the way for authoritarian leaders to position themselves as saviors.

Fascism's rise in the 20th century was not inevitable—it was the result of specific conditions, exploited by leaders who saw opportunity in crisis. By understanding these conditions, we can identify the warning signs of authoritarian movements and take steps to prevent history from repeating itself.

In the next chapter, we will examine how these forces converge in the creation of a "cult of personality," the centerpiece of fascist movements, and their reliance on charismatic leaders to cement power.

## Chapter 4: Early American Flirtations with Fascism

While the United States is often viewed as a bastion of democracy, its history is not immune to flirtations with fascist ideologies. In the early 20th century, movements like the German-American Bund and the America First Committee reflected themes of authoritarianism, nationalism, and exclusion that paralleled the rise of fascism in Europe. Prominent figures like Charles Lindbergh and Father Charles Coughlin amplified these ideas, cultivating a climate of fear, resentment, and division that echoed fascist rhetoric abroad.

## The German-American Bund: A Fascist Outpost on American Soil

In the 1930s, as Adolf Hitler consolidated power in Germany, the German-American Bund emerged as a vocal supporter of the Nazi regime within the United States. Headed by Fritz Kuhn, a naturalized American citizen of German descent, the Bund promoted Nazi ideology, including antisemitism, ultranationalism, and loyalty to Hitler. The organization sought to align German-Americans with the Nazi cause, portraying itself as a cultural and political advocate for German heritage.

The Bund held rallies across the United States, the most infamous of which took place in Madison Square Garden in 1939. Thousands gathered under swastika banners alongside American flags, listening to speeches that denounced Jews, communists, and President Franklin D. Roosevelt as threats to American values. The rally culminated in violence when protestors clashed with Bund supporters, highlighting the volatile intersection of fascist sympathies and public resistance.

Though the Bund failed to gain widespread support, its existence exposed the vulnerabilities of American society to fascist propaganda. The group's ability to operate openly, recruit members, and spread its ideology demonstrated how easily fascist ideas could take root, even in a democracy.

## The America First Committee: Isolationism with a Fascist Underpinning

Founded in 1940, the America First Committee initially framed itself as a nonpartisan organization advocating for U.S. neutrality in World War II. However, its rhetoric and leadership often mirrored the xenophobia and authoritarianism associated with fascism. With figures like aviator Charles Lindbergh as its public face, America First gained significant traction, boasting nearly 800,000 members at its peak.

Lindbergh, a national hero for his transatlantic flight, became a polarizing figure due to his outspoken admiration for Nazi Germany. In speeches and writings, he praised Germany's military strength and expressed thinly veiled antisemitic views, blaming Jewish influence for pushing the United States toward war. In a 1941 speech in Des Moines, Iowa, Lindbergh stated, "The three most important groups who have been pressing this country toward war are the British, the Jewish, and the Roosevelt administration."

The America First Committee capitalized on fears of foreign entanglements and economic instability, presenting isolationism as a patriotic duty. While not explicitly fascist, its rhetoric echoed the themes of ultranationalism and exclusion that were central to fascist movements abroad. The committee disbanded after the attack on Pearl Harbor in 1941, but its legacy of divisive, exclusionary politics persisted.

---

## Father Charles Coughlin: The Radio Priest of Hate

Another prominent figure in America's flirtation with fascism was Father Charles Coughlin, a Catholic priest whose radio broadcasts reached millions of listeners during the 1930s. Initially a supporter of President Roosevelt and the New Deal, Coughlin grew increasingly radical, using his platform to spread antisemitic conspiracies, promote authoritarian governance, and criticize democracy as weak and ineffective.

Coughlin's broadcasts frequently echoed the rhetoric of

European fascists. He blamed Jews for economic woes, portrayed communism as a global Jewish conspiracy, and called for the nationalization of industries under a strong central authority. His magazine, *Social Justice*, published excerpts from *The Protocols of the Elders of Zion*, a notorious antisemitic forgery that claimed to outline a Jewish plot for world domination.

Though Coughlin's influence waned after the onset of World War II, his ability to mobilize millions of Americans demonstrated how easily fascist themes could resonate within a population grappling with economic uncertainty and social change.

## The Fragility of American Democracy

The German-American Bund, the America First Committee, and Father Coughlin's movement all highlighted the fragility of American democracy during times of crisis. These movements revealed how economic hardship, cultural anxieties, and charismatic leaders could be exploited to spread authoritarian and exclusionary ideologies.

While none of these movements succeeded in establishing fascism in the United States, they laid bare the vulnerabilities of a divided society. They also underscored the importance of vigilance: fascism need not emerge as a fully formed regime; it often begins with the normalization of extremist ideas and the gradual erosion of democratic values.

## Lessons for Today

The early 20th century provides a cautionary tale about the

susceptibility of democratic societies to fascist ideologies. The rise of movements like the German-American Bund and America First Committee illustrates how fear, economic instability, and charismatic figures can pave the way for authoritarianism.

In our current era, echoes of these movements are apparent in the rhetoric of exclusion, the undermining of democratic norms, and the targeting of marginalized groups. Understanding these historical precedents is vital to recognizing and resisting their modern parallels.

In the next chapter, we will explore how these dynamics evolve into the cult of personality that anchors fascist movements, examining the role of charismatic leaders in consolidating power and shaping the narratives that sustain authoritarianism.

## Part II: Modern Parallels

## Chapter 5: The Cult of Personality

At the heart of every fascist movement lies the cult of personality—a phenomenon in which a charismatic leader becomes the embodiment of the nation's hopes, fears, and identity. This dynamic, both seductive and dangerous, allows leaders to consolidate power, suppress dissent, and rewrite societal narratives. By examining historical examples and their modern counterparts, we can better understand how such leaders rise and why their influence endangers democracy.

## The Anatomy of a Cult of Personality

A cult of personality does not arise by chance; it is deliberately constructed. It begins with a leader who understands how to project strength and charisma, often using grandiose language to frame themselves as saviors of a struggling nation. Through propaganda, selective storytelling, and the suppression of opposition, these figures create an aura of infallibility, fostering unwavering loyalty among their followers.

Historically, Adolf Hitler in Germany and Benito Mussolini in Italy mastered this art. Both men cultivated public personas that transcended ordinary political leadership. They positioned themselves as the only individuals capable of restoring their nations to greatness, using highly visible gestures—mass rallies, dramatic speeches, and media portrayals—to reinforce their image as larger-than-life figures.

Modern charismatic leaders, while operating in different contexts, often follow similar playbooks. They craft narratives of personal sacrifice, strength, and vision, portraying themselves as singularly capable of addressing national crises. Whether through social media, television, or public appearances, these leaders use modern platforms to amplify their personas, drawing comparisons to historical figures who leveraged radio, newspapers, and film.

## Historical Parallels: From Hitler to Mussolini

### Adolf Hitler: The Messiah of the Reich

In Nazi Germany, Hitler's rise hinged on his ability to present himself as the savior of a nation humiliated by the Treaty of Versailles and devastated by economic collapse. Through relentless propaganda orchestrated by Joseph Goebbels, Hitler was depicted as a man of the people, a tireless leader who understood Germany's plight and could deliver redemption.

His speeches were meticulously crafted to evoke emotion, combining promises of economic revival with appeals to national pride and unity. Hitler's charismatic presence at Nazi rallies, surrounded by flags and cheering crowds, reinforced his centrality to Germany's destiny. His voice—commanding, urgent, and theatrical—became synonymous with the Nazi movement, making dissent nearly unthinkable for many Germans.

### Benito Mussolini: The Visionary of Rome

Mussolini's cult of personality similarly relied on spectacle. He cultivated an image of invincibility, styling himself as the modern incarnation of a Roman emperor. Through newspapers, radio broadcasts, and staged public events, Mussolini projected strength and decisiveness.

His ability to control media narratives allowed him to silence critics and manipulate public perception. Mussolini's slogans, such as *"Mussolini is always right,"* reinforced the idea that he was the ultimate authority—a figure who embodied the will of the Italian people.

## Modern Parallels: Charisma in the Digital Age

While modern leaders operate in vastly different technological and cultural landscapes, the tactics of building a cult of personality remain remarkably consistent. Today's political figures use social media, 24-hour news cycles, and carefully curated public appearances to command attention and loyalty.

### Selective Comparisons

- **Donald Trump**: Trump's presidency relied heavily on the construction of a cult of personality. His rallies became events where he reinforced his brand as a leader fighting for "forgotten Americans." Like historical fascists, Trump weaponized media to dominate narratives, casting himself as a victim of conspiracies and the only one capable of "making America great again." His use of slogans, inflammatory language, and polarizing rhetoric mirrors tactics employed by figures like Mussolini and Hitler.
- **Vladimir Putin**: In Russia, Putin has cultivated an image of strength and resilience, positioning himself as a defender of Russian values and a bulwark against Western influence. State-controlled media reinforces this image, portraying him as a heroic figure who embodies Russian pride and stability.

### Media as Amplifier

Social media platforms, in particular, have revolutionized the cult of personality. Leaders can bypass traditional gatekeepers and speak directly to their followers, often using platforms to stoke division and loyalty simultaneously. While Hitler and Mussolini relied on state-controlled media, modern leaders exploit algorithms designed to amplify emotionally charged content, creating echo chambers that reinforce their narratives.

## The Role of Fear and Division

A cult of personality thrives on fear and division. Leaders craft an "us versus them" dynamic, portraying themselves as protectors of the virtuous majority against dangerous outsiders or internal enemies. This tactic solidifies their base while silencing dissent.

- **Historical Context**: Hitler's demonization of Jews and communists framed them as existential threats to German society, justifying his authoritarian measures.
- **Modern Echoes**: Today, similar tactics are used to target immigrants, political opponents, and marginalized groups, with leaders often casting themselves as defenders of traditional values against perceived threats.

## Dangers of the Cult of Personality

The cult of personality erodes democratic norms by centralizing power and stifling dissent. When loyalty to a leader supersedes loyalty to democratic principles, institutions become tools of the leader's will rather than safeguards of the public good.

This dynamic also isolates followers from reality. The leader's rhetoric becomes the sole lens through which they interpret events, creating a closed feedback loop that discourages critical thinking. As history has shown, this level of control often leads to devastating consequences, from human rights abuses to the collapse of democratic systems.

## Lessons for Resistance

To counter the cult of personality, it is essential to:

1. **Promote Institutional Strength**: Support independent media, judiciary systems, and checks on executive power to prevent the over-centralization of authority.
2. **Encourage Critical Thinking**: Equip citizens with tools to identify manipulation and propaganda, fostering a culture of skepticism and inquiry.
3. **Celebrate Collective Leadership**: Highlight the importance of collaborative governance over individual hero worship, reinforcing the value of democratic principles.

By understanding the mechanics of the cult of personality, we can recognize its manifestations in modern politics and resist its corrosive effects on democracy.

In the next chapter, we will explore how nationalism and grievance politics intertwine to further solidify authoritarian movements, creating a narrative that binds citizens through exclusion and shared resentment.

## Chapter 6: Nationalism and Grievance Politics

Nationalism, when wielded as a unifying force, can inspire pride and solidarity among a population. However, when paired with grievance politics, it becomes a powerful tool for authoritarian leaders to divide and conquer. Fascist movements have historically exploited economic and cultural grievances, transforming legitimate frustrations into weapons of division and exclusion. By identifying scapegoats and promoting a singular vision of national identity, they galvanize support while marginalizing those who do not conform.

## Exploiting Economic Grievances

Economic instability has always been fertile ground for authoritarianism. In the wake of World War I, the Great Depression, and other crises, fascist leaders in Europe seized on widespread discontent to frame their movements as solutions to financial despair.

- **Germany's Economic Collapse**: Following the Treaty of Versailles, Germany's economy spiraled into hyperinflation and unemployment. Adolf Hitler channeled the anger of the German people, blaming Jews, communists, and foreign powers for the nation's decline. His promises to rebuild the economy, restore national pride, and punish those responsible resonated deeply with a population desperate for hope.
- **Italy's Post-War Turmoil**: In Italy, Benito Mussolini capitalized on high unemployment and social unrest. He presented fascism as the cure for the failings of liberal democracy and the chaos of class struggle, uniting disparate groups under the banner of nationalism.

These leaders did not solve economic crises so much as redirect blame, using grievances to reinforce hierarchies and justify authoritarian control.

## Cultural Grievances and Identity Politics

Fascist movements also manipulate cultural grievances, portraying changes in societal norms as threats to national identity. This tactic creates a framework of "us versus them," where the "other" becomes the root cause of societal decline.

- **The Myth of Cultural Purity**: Fascist rhetoric often idealizes a homogenous past, casting diversity, immigration, and progressive values as corrosive forces. In Nazi Germany, the concept of Aryan racial purity was central to Hitler's platform, justifying policies of exclusion, violence, and genocide.
- **Gender and Traditional Values**: Movements like Franco's Spain and Mussolini's Italy promoted patriarchal norms, portraying feminism, LGBTQ+ rights, and shifts in gender roles as betrayals of national traditions. These narratives were used to suppress dissent and reinforce social hierarchies.

## Modern Echoes: America First and Grievance Politics

In contemporary politics, these patterns persist, particularly in rhetoric like "America First," which echoes fascist themes of exclusionary nationalism and grievance exploitation.

### Economic Grievances

- **Globalization as a Scapegoat**: Modern nationalist movements often frame globalization as a threat to domestic jobs and industries, blaming foreign countries, immigrants, or international agreements for economic hardships. This narrative, while oversimplified, resonates with populations experiencing economic insecurity.

- **Widening Inequality**: Economic grievances are exacerbated by rising inequality, which nationalist leaders use to foster resentment toward elites or minority groups, framing them as undeserving beneficiaries of the system.

## Cultural Grievances

- **Immigration and Identity**: Rhetoric around immigration often mirrors the cultural purity arguments of historical fascism. In the United States, immigrants are frequently portrayed as threats to jobs, safety, and national values, fueling policies aimed at exclusion and enforcement.
- **Reviving the "Mythic Past"**: The call to "Make America Great Again" is deeply rooted in grievance politics, invoking an undefined golden age where traditional values allegedly reigned supreme. This message capitalizes on cultural anxieties about changing demographics, progressive social movements, and global interconnectedness.

---

## The Mechanics of Division

At the core of grievance politics is the deliberate fostering of division. Authoritarian leaders use three primary tactics:

1. **Identifying Scapegoats**: By blaming societal ills on specific groups—immigrants, minorities, intellectuals, or

the media—leaders deflect criticism from systemic issues and their own failures.

2. **Polarizing Society**: Fascist rhetoric reduces complex problems to binary choices, creating a dichotomy of patriots versus enemies. This polarization solidifies support among the base while alienating dissenters.

3. **Eroding Trust**: Nationalist leaders undermine trust in institutions, framing them as corrupt or out of touch. This tactic isolates citizens from objective sources of truth, making them more reliant on the leader's narrative.

---

## The Dangerous Allure of Grievance Politics

Grievance politics appeals to the human desire for clarity and control. In times of uncertainty, it offers simple explanations and direct targets for frustration. However, this clarity comes at a cost. By fostering division and scapegoating, grievance politics undermines social cohesion, erodes trust in democratic institutions, and paves the way for authoritarian rule.

---

## Lessons for Resistance

To counter the corrosive effects of grievance politics, it is essential to:

1. **Reframe the Narrative**: Promote messages of unity and shared responsibility, emphasizing the complexity of societal challenges rather than assigning blame.

2. **Address Underlying Inequalities**: Reducing economic and social disparities can defuse the grievances that authoritarian leaders exploit.
3. **Strengthen Institutions**: Building public trust in democratic systems and the rule of law can reduce susceptibility to divisive rhetoric.

Grievance politics may appear powerful, but its foundation is brittle. By fostering inclusion, empathy, and critical thinking, democratic societies can withstand the forces that seek to divide them.

In the next chapter, we will explore how authoritarian movements undermine democratic institutions, analyzing the tactics used to erode checks and balances and consolidate power.

## Chapter 7: Undermining Democratic Institutions

Democratic institutions are the backbone of free societies, providing checks on power, protecting individual rights, and ensuring accountability. For authoritarian leaders, these institutions are obstacles to control and must be weakened or dismantled. Historically, fascist regimes have systematically undermined courts, elections, and independent governing bodies to consolidate power. Today, similar tactics are evident in modern political trends, from questioning election integrity to eroding judicial independence.

# Historical Playbook: Destroying Democratic Foundations

Fascist movements of the 20th century showed a clear pattern in dismantling democratic institutions. Their tactics were calculated, gradual, and disguised as reforms to restore order and efficiency.

## Dismantling Courts

- **Germany under Hitler**: One of Adolf Hitler's first moves after becoming chancellor in 1933 was the passage of the *Reichstag Fire Decree*. This decree suspended constitutional rights and allowed the Nazi regime to imprison political opponents without due process. The judiciary, once a cornerstone of the Weimar Republic, was transformed into an arm of the Nazi Party, rubber-stamping policies that facilitated persecution and genocide.
- **Italy under Mussolini**: Benito Mussolini similarly weakened judicial independence by appointing loyalists to key positions. Judges who opposed his regime were removed or silenced, ensuring that the courts would uphold fascist policies without resistance.

## Subverting Elections

- **Germany**: The Enabling Act of 1933, passed under duress and with widespread intimidation of opposition politicians, effectively dismantled parliamentary democracy in Germany. It granted Hitler legislative powers, eliminating the need for free elections and legislative oversight.

- **Spain under Franco**: Francisco Franco's regime maintained the veneer of elections but controlled the process to ensure outcomes favorable to his authoritarian rule. Opposition parties were banned, and the electorate had no real choice.

## Eliminating Checks on Power

- Fascist regimes systematically neutralized legislative bodies, independent watchdogs, and political opposition. By controlling or abolishing these entities, leaders ensured they faced no institutional resistance to their policies.

## Modern Trends: Eroding Trust in Institutions

While outright dismantling of institutions is rare in modern democracies, authoritarian-leaning leaders employ more subtle tactics to weaken them. These include delegitimizing courts, casting doubt on election results, and undermining the independence of democratic bodies.

## Questioning Election Integrity

One of the most concerning trends in modern politics is the deliberate undermining of public confidence in elections:

- **United States**: In the wake of the 2020 presidential election, efforts to question the legitimacy of results reached unprecedented levels. False claims of widespread voter fraud and attempts to overturn certified results shook public trust in the electoral process. Events like the January 6, 2021, attack on the Capitol highlighted the real-world dangers of such rhetoric.

- **Global Parallels**: Similar tactics have been employed in countries like Brazil, where Jair Bolsonaro preemptively questioned the validity of elections he ultimately lost, and Hungary, where Viktor Orbán has manipulated electoral systems to ensure his continued dominance.

## Undermining Judicial Independence

Judiciaries are another target for modern authoritarian-leaning leaders:

- **Poland**: The ruling Law and Justice Party (PiS) has systematically weakened judicial independence by passing laws that allow political leaders to appoint and dismiss judges. This has sparked widespread protests and criticism from the European Union.
- **United States**: Attacks on the judiciary as "biased" or "activist" have become commonplace in political rhetoric, eroding public trust in courts as impartial arbiters of the law.

## Weakening Checks and Balances

Modern leaders often exploit legal loopholes or push the boundaries of institutional norms to consolidate power:

- **Russia under Vladimir Putin**: Putin has used constitutional amendments to extend his rule, while sidelining political opponents through legal and extrajudicial means.

- **Turkey under Recep Tayyip Erdoğan**: Erdoğan's government has purged thousands of civil servants, academics, and judges, effectively silencing dissent and consolidating control over state institutions.

## The Tactics of Undermining Institutions

1. **Delegitimization**: Leaders attack institutions as corrupt, ineffective, or biased to justify their actions. For example, branding courts as "activist" or elections as "rigged" erodes public confidence and paves the way for further interference.
2. **Incremental Change**: Rather than outright abolishing institutions, authoritarian leaders make gradual changes—packing courts, amending constitutions, or passing restrictive laws—that weaken institutional independence over time.
3. **Concentration of Power**: Shifting authority from independent bodies to executive control consolidates power in the hands of a single leader or party.

## Consequences of Eroding Institutions

The weakening of democratic institutions has profound and far-reaching effects:

- **Loss of Accountability**: Without independent courts or watchdogs, leaders face little scrutiny, enabling corruption and abuse of power.
- **Erosion of Public Trust**: Attacks on elections and courts undermine confidence in democracy, leading to apathy, polarization, and disengagement among citizens.
- **Normalization of Authoritarianism**: As institutions lose their independence, authoritarian measures become normalized, paving the way for further encroachments on freedoms and rights.

---

## Lessons for Resistance

1. **Protect Electoral Integrity**: Ensuring free and fair elections is paramount. This includes safeguarding voting systems, combating disinformation, and promoting transparency in the electoral process.
2. **Strengthen Judicial Independence**: Courts must remain impartial and insulated from political interference. Supporting judicial independence through laws and advocacy is essential to maintaining checks on power.
3. **Uphold Institutional Norms**: Civil society, media, and opposition parties play crucial roles in holding leaders accountable and preserving institutional integrity.

By understanding the tactics used to undermine democratic institutions, we can better defend against their erosion. In the next chapter, we will explore the role of propaganda in facilitating authoritarian rule, examining how disinformation and media manipulation create a controlled narrative that supports the consolidation of power.

## Chapter 8: The Role of Propaganda

Propaganda is the engine of authoritarian movements, enabling leaders to control narratives, manipulate perceptions, and galvanize loyalty. From the radio broadcasts of the early 20th century to the algorithms of modern social media platforms, the methods of disseminating propaganda have evolved, but their purpose remains the same: to consolidate power and suppress dissent. By examining historical examples and their modern equivalents, we can understand how propaganda serves as a tool of control and why it is so effective in shaping public opinion.

## Propaganda in the Fascist Era

Fascist regimes of the 20th century mastered the art of propaganda, using emerging communication technologies to create powerful narratives that justified their policies and demonized their enemies.

### The Nazi Propaganda Machine

In Nazi Germany, Joseph Goebbels, the Minister of Propaganda, revolutionized the use of media as a tool for authoritarian control. The Nazi propaganda machine operated on multiple fronts:

- **Film and Radio**: Films like *Triumph of the Will* glorified Adolf Hitler and the Nazi Party, presenting them as the saviors of Germany. Radio broadcasts, which reached millions of households, reinforced messages of national pride and racial superiority.
- **Print Media**: Newspapers like *Der Stürmer* spread antisemitic conspiracy theories and dehumanized Jews, creating public support for policies of exclusion and violence.
- **Symbolism and Spectacle**: Mass rallies, banners, and uniforms created a visual language of power and unity, reinforcing the regime's dominance and making opposition appear futile.

Goebbels famously stated, "A lie told once remains a lie, but a lie told a thousand times becomes the truth." This philosophy underscores the repetitive nature of propaganda, designed to erode critical thinking and create a shared reality dictated by the regime.

## Mussolini's Media Domination

In Italy, Benito Mussolini similarly used propaganda to cultivate his image as a heroic and infallible leader. Through state-controlled media, Mussolini suppressed dissenting voices and portrayed fascism as the only path to Italian greatness. The regime's propaganda celebrated the Roman Empire as a symbol of Italy's destiny, reinforcing the mythic past to inspire loyalty.

## The Evolution of Propaganda: From Broadcasts to Algorithms

While 20th-century propaganda relied on centralized control of mass media, modern disinformation campaigns are decentralized, pervasive, and amplified by digital technology.

### Social Media Algorithms

Social media platforms like Facebook, Twitter, and YouTube have become the new battlegrounds for propaganda. Unlike traditional media, these platforms use algorithms to prioritize content that generates engagement—often sensational or divisive material. Authoritarian movements exploit this by:

- **Spreading Disinformation**: False narratives, conspiracy theories, and misleading content are shared widely, creating confusion and eroding trust in reliable sources.
- **Amplifying Division**: Algorithms amplify polarizing content, creating echo chambers where individuals are exposed only to viewpoints that reinforce their beliefs.
- **Manufacturing Consent**: By flooding platforms with propaganda, authoritarian actors shape public discourse, making their narratives appear dominant or inevitable.

## Deepfakes and Manipulated Media

Advancements in technology, such as deepfakes and AI-generated content, have added a new layer of complexity to propaganda. These tools can create hyper-realistic but false images and videos, further undermining trust in what is real and what is fabricated.

## Disinformation Campaigns

State-sponsored disinformation campaigns, such as those attributed to Russia, use social media to sow discord in other countries. During the 2016 U.S. presidential election, Russian operatives used fake accounts to amplify divisive issues, weakening trust in democratic processes.

## Why Propaganda Works

Propaganda is effective because it taps into fundamental aspects of human psychology:

1. **Emotional Appeal**: Propaganda often bypasses rational thought, targeting emotions like fear, anger, and pride to elicit immediate reactions.
2. **Repetition**: Repeated exposure to a message, even if false, increases its perceived credibility—a phenomenon known as the "illusory truth effect."
3. **Group Identity**: Propaganda exploits the human desire for belonging by framing issues in terms of "us versus them." This fosters loyalty to the in-group and hostility toward outsiders.
4. **Information Overload**: In the digital age, the sheer volume of information makes it difficult for individuals to discern credible sources, leaving them vulnerable to manipulation.

## The Consequences of Propaganda

Unchecked propaganda has far-reaching consequences for society:

- **Polarization**: By amplifying divisions, propaganda creates a fragmented society where constructive dialogue becomes nearly impossible.
- **Erosion of Truth**: The deliberate spread of falsehoods undermines trust in facts and institutions, paving the way for authoritarian control.
- **Dehumanization**: Propaganda often targets specific groups, portraying them as threats to national identity or security. This dehumanization justifies exclusion, violence, and systemic discrimination.

## Modern Examples of Propaganda in Action

### 2020 U.S. Election Disinformation

In the aftermath of the 2020 U.S. presidential election, false claims of voter fraud spread rapidly on social media, fueled by both individuals and coordinated campaigns. These narratives undermined trust in the electoral process, culminating in the January 6, 2021, attack on the Capitol. The event demonstrated the tangible dangers of propaganda when amplified in a polarized environment.

### Authoritarian Narratives in China

The Chinese government uses a combination of censorship and propaganda to control narratives about its policies, such as the treatment of Uyghur Muslims and the Hong Kong protests. By suppressing dissenting voices and flooding social media with state-approved content, the government shapes domestic and international perceptions of its actions.

### Lessons for Resistance

1. **Media Literacy**: Educating the public on how to identify and critically evaluate propaganda is crucial. Media literacy programs can empower individuals to discern credible information from disinformation.
2. **Transparency in Platforms**: Social media companies must take responsibility for their role in amplifying

propaganda. Greater transparency in algorithmic decision-making and stricter regulation of false content are necessary to combat disinformation.

3. **Supporting Independent Media**: Strengthening independent journalism provides a counterbalance to state-sponsored propaganda, ensuring that diverse perspectives are represented.

Propaganda has evolved, but its purpose remains the same: to control narratives, suppress dissent, and consolidate power. By understanding how it operates, we can develop tools to resist its influence and safeguard the principles of democracy.

In the next chapter, we will examine the economic and social conditions that enable authoritarianism, analyzing how inequality, instability, and fear create fertile ground for fascist ideologies to take hold.

## Chapter 9: Creating Us vs. Them

At the core of authoritarian and fascist movements lies the strategy of division, manifesting as the creation of an "us versus them" narrative. By framing one group as the rightful heirs to a nation's identity and prosperity, while dehumanizing others as threats or scapegoats, these movements foster unity through exclusion. This tactic, rooted in fear and resentment, has been a hallmark of fascist regimes throughout history and continues to shape contemporary politics.

# The Historical Blueprint of Division

Fascist leaders have historically relied on the "us versus them" dynamic to consolidate power and justify oppressive policies. By positioning minority groups as existential threats, they redirected societal grievances away from structural issues and toward easily identifiable scapegoats.

## Germany: The Nazi Narrative

Adolf Hitler and the Nazi Party epitomized this tactic by targeting Jews, portraying them as the root of Germany's post-World War I struggles. Nazi propaganda depicted Jews as parasitic, disloyal, and conspiratorial, accusing them of undermining German society. This dehumanization justified increasingly oppressive policies, culminating in the Holocaust.

- **Dehumanization through Propaganda**: Nazi-controlled media published grotesque caricatures of Jews, likening them to vermin and disease. This imagery made it easier for ordinary Germans to accept, or even participate in, atrocities.
- **Defining the "True German"**: The Nazis framed Aryan Germans as the epitome of cultural and racial purity, contrasting them with Jewish "others" who were cast as corrupting influences.

## Italy: Targeting Political and Ethnic Minorities

In Mussolini's Italy, the "us versus them" narrative was initially directed at political enemies like socialists and communists, who were labeled as threats to national unity. Over time, this expanded to include ethnic minorities, particularly Slavs, who were vilified as inferior and uncivilized.

- **Exclusion through Law**: Mussolini's regime implemented racial laws mirroring those in Nazi Germany, further institutionalizing the division between "us" and "them."

---

## Contemporary Parallels: Division in Modern Politics

In the 21st century, the "us versus them" strategy continues to shape political rhetoric and policies. While the targets and platforms have shifted, the underlying dynamics remain consistent.

## Immigrants as Scapegoats

Immigration has become a central issue in modern divisive politics, with immigrants often portrayed as threats to jobs, culture, and safety.

- **United States**: The rhetoric of building a border wall and characterizing immigrants as "rapists" and "criminals" reflects a deliberate strategy to stoke fear and division. Policies like family separation at the border further dehumanize immigrants, treating them as less than human.
- **Europe**: Anti-immigration sentiment has fueled the rise of far-right parties in countries like Hungary, France, and the United Kingdom. Leaders like Viktor Orbán have

used the rhetoric of "defending European culture" to justify restrictive immigration policies and attacks on multiculturalism.

## Targeting Religious Minorities

Religious minorities often bear the brunt of exclusionary rhetoric, framed as incompatible with the dominant culture.

- **India**: Hindu nationalist rhetoric, under leaders like Narendra Modi, has increasingly marginalized Muslims, portraying them as a threat to India's identity and stability.
- **China**: The Chinese government's treatment of Uyghur Muslims, including mass internment and cultural erasure, is a stark example of dehumanization on a systemic scale.

## Weaponizing Gender and Sexuality

Marginalized groups based on gender and sexuality are also frequent targets of the "us versus them" narrative.

- **Anti-LGBTQ+ Policies**: Rhetoric framing LGBTQ+ rights as a threat to family values or religious freedom is used to justify discriminatory policies, such as banning same-sex marriage or criminalizing gender-affirming care.
- **Feminism as a "Threat"**: Authoritarian movements often position feminist progress as an attack on traditional family structures, casting empowered women as adversaries to cultural norms.

## The Mechanics of Division

The "us versus them" dynamic relies on specific psychological and rhetorical strategies to gain traction:

1. **Fear-Mongering**: Leaders amplify fears of societal change or collapse, linking these anxieties to the presence or actions of minority groups.
2. **Simplistic Narratives**: Complex issues, such as economic disparity or political instability, are reduced to binary explanations, where one group is the source of all problems.
3. **Dehumanization**: Language and imagery that liken marginalized groups to animals, diseases, or criminals strip them of humanity, making oppression or violence more palatable.
4. **In-Group Identity**: Propaganda emphasizes the moral superiority and victimhood of the "us" group, fostering loyalty and justifying exclusion.

## The Politics of Exclusion and Identity

The "us versus them" narrative thrives on identity politics, but not the kind that seeks to celebrate diversity. Instead, it reinforces a singular identity as the only legitimate one, excluding all others.

- **National Identity**: Claims of cultural or racial purity are used to exclude immigrants and minorities.

- **Religious Identity**: Dominant religions are framed as synonymous with national identity, marginalizing those of other faiths.
- **Cultural Hierarchies**: Traditional gender roles and sexual norms are upheld as cornerstones of society, casting LGBTQ+ people and feminists as threats to stability.

This exclusionary politics serves a dual purpose: uniting the majority under a common identity while suppressing dissent by labeling it as disloyal or subversive.

## The Consequences of Division

The "us versus them" narrative corrodes the foundations of democracy and human rights:

- **Erosion of Social Trust**: Division undermines trust between groups, making cooperation and mutual understanding impossible.
- **Justification for Oppression**: Dehumanization provides a pretext for discriminatory laws, surveillance, and violence.
- **Radicalization**: The rhetoric of division can inspire extremist actions, from hate crimes to terrorism, as individuals feel emboldened to act against perceived threats.

## Lessons for Resistance

To counter the "us versus them" dynamic, societies must actively promote inclusivity and empathy:

1. **Foster Dialogue**: Creating spaces for open, respectful conversation between groups can break down stereotypes and build mutual understanding.
2. **Humanize the Other**: Media and education must focus on telling the stories of marginalized groups in ways that emphasize shared humanity.
3. **Challenge Divisive Narratives**: Politicians, educators, and activists must work to expose and dismantle propaganda that seeks to divide.

---

The "us versus them" narrative is a powerful weapon in the authoritarian arsenal, but it can be resisted through intentional efforts to foster inclusivity and solidarity. In the next chapter, we will explore how authoritarian leaders weaponize "law and order" rhetoric to suppress dissent and solidify control.

# Chapter 10: Law and Order as a Weapon

The promise of "law and order" has long been used as a rallying cry by authoritarian leaders to justify the suppression of dissent, the erosion of rights, and the marginalization of vulnerable groups. While the rhetoric invokes safety and stability, its implementation often serves as a tool for control, targeting opposition movements, minorities, and any perceived threats to the ruling regime. Historically, fascist regimes weaponized law and order to consolidate power, and contemporary parallels in criminal justice and immigration policies demonstrate how this tactic continues to be employed in modern societies.

## Historical Use of "Law and Order" in Fascist Regimes

### Nazi Germany: Laws of Repression

In Nazi Germany, "law and order" became synonymous with control and persecution. The regime enacted sweeping legislation to criminalize dissent and legitimize state violence:

- **Reichstag Fire Decree (1933)**: Framed as a response to the alleged communist threat following the Reichstag fire, this decree suspended civil liberties, allowing for arbitrary arrests and the suppression of opposition parties.
- **Nuremberg Laws (1935)**: These laws institutionalized racial discrimination, stripping Jews of citizenship and legal protections under the guise of maintaining social order.

By framing these measures as necessary for public safety, the Nazis silenced critics, dismantled democratic structures, and enacted policies that paved the way for genocide.

### Italy under Mussolini: Policing Opposition

Benito Mussolini used law and order rhetoric to justify the repression of political opponents and social movements:

- **Criminalization of Dissent**: Mussolini's regime passed laws that banned socialist and communist parties, labeling them threats to national stability.
- **Secret Police**: The OVRA (Organization for Vigilance and Repression of Anti-Fascism) monitored and suppressed

opposition through surveillance, arrests, and extrajudicial actions.

These measures were couched in language that appealed to public fears of chaos, portraying Mussolini as the only leader capable of restoring stability.

## The Rhetoric of Fear and Stability

The effectiveness of the law and order narrative lies in its appeal to fear and its promise of safety. Leaders frame dissent, diversity, or societal change as chaos and disorder, positioning themselves as protectors of the public. This tactic not only suppresses opposition but also garners widespread support from citizens who perceive the crackdown as a necessary defense against instability.

## Modern Parallels: Law and Order in Contemporary Politics

### Criminal Justice as a Tool of Control

In modern democracies, the rhetoric of law and order often targets marginalized communities, disproportionately enforcing policies that perpetuate inequality:

- **United States**: The "War on Drugs," initiated in the 1980s, disproportionately targeted Black and Latino communities, leading to mass incarceration. More recently, protests against police violence have been met with militarized responses under the guise of maintaining order.
- **Brazil**: Jair Bolsonaro's administration used law and order rhetoric to justify aggressive policing in favelas,

disproportionately affecting low-income communities and perpetuating cycles of violence.

These policies are often framed as essential for public safety, but they primarily serve to reinforce existing power structures and silence demands for systemic change.

**Immigration and Border Control**

Law and order rhetoric is also weaponized in immigration policy, portraying migrants as threats to national security:

- **United States**: Policies like family separation and "zero tolerance" border enforcement have been justified as measures to uphold the law. The framing of migrants as criminals fuels public support for harsh measures, despite their humanitarian costs.
- **Europe**: Anti-immigration rhetoric has led to increased border militarization and the criminalization of asylum seekers in countries like Hungary and Italy.

By casting immigration as a crisis, leaders deflect attention from structural issues, fostering fear and division to bolster their political agendas.

## The Role of Policing and Surveillance

Modern authoritarian-leaning governments use expanded policing powers and surveillance to stifle dissent under the pretense of maintaining law and order:

- **Hong Kong**: In response to pro-democracy protests, China imposed a national security law that criminalized dissent, allowing for mass arrests and the suppression of political expression.

- **Russia**: Vladimir Putin's government uses surveillance and anti-protest laws to silence opposition, framing activists as threats to public stability.

These measures echo historical examples, illustrating how law and order rhetoric can be weaponized to maintain control and suppress resistance.

## The Consequences of Weaponized Law and Order

The misuse of law and order rhetoric has far-reaching implications for democracy and human rights:

1. **Erosion of Civil Liberties**: Expanded policing powers and repressive laws undermine fundamental freedoms, such as speech and assembly.
2. **Normalization of Oppression**: Targeting marginalized groups creates a culture of fear and compliance, discouraging resistance to authoritarian policies.
3. **Entrenchment of Inequality**: Discriminatory enforcement of laws perpetuates systemic inequities, marginalizing communities and eroding trust in institutions.

## Resisting the Weaponization of Law and Order

To counter the misuse of law and order rhetoric, it is essential to:

1.  **Demand Accountability**: Strengthen oversight mechanisms for law enforcement and judicial systems to prevent abuse of power.
2.  **Promote Equity**: Address systemic biases in criminal justice and immigration policies to ensure fair treatment for all.
3.  **Foster Public Awareness**: Educate citizens about the dangers of sacrificing civil liberties for perceived security, emphasizing the importance of maintaining democratic principles.

The rhetoric of law and order, when weaponized, becomes a tool of authoritarianism, undermining democracy and perpetuating inequality. By recognizing its misuse, we can resist the fear-driven narratives that seek to erode our freedoms. In the next chapter, we will examine the economic and social conditions that create fertile ground for authoritarian ideologies, exploring how inequality and instability fuel the rise of such movements.

## Part III: Economic and Social Conditions

## Chapter 11: The Role of Economic Anxiety

Economic anxiety is a potent force in shaping political landscapes. When individuals and communities face financial insecurity, fear and frustration can lead to a search for simple explanations and immediate solutions. Authoritarian movements and leaders have historically exploited these conditions, channeling economic grievances into support for extremist ideologies. By examining historical and modern examples, we can understand how economic fears are leveraged to foster division and consolidate power.

---

## Economic Anxiety as a Fertile Ground for Extremism

Economic instability disrupts not only material well-being but also social and psychological security. Financial hardship creates a sense of vulnerability and a loss of control, driving people to seek stability, even at the cost of democratic principles. This environment is particularly susceptible to narratives that identify scapegoats and promise swift restoration of economic order.

---

## Historical Examples: Exploiting Economic Fears

### Post-World War I Germany

The Treaty of Versailles plunged Germany into economic chaos, imposing heavy reparations that crippled the nation's economy. The Great Depression exacerbated these conditions, with unemployment soaring to 30% and millions losing their livelihoods.

- **Scapegoating**: Adolf Hitler and the Nazi Party redirected public anger toward Jews, communists, and other minority groups, framing them as the cause of Germany's economic decline. This narrative not only unified disillusioned Germans but also justified discriminatory policies.

- **False Promises of Prosperity**: The Nazis promised economic recovery through rearmament and public works projects, offering the population a sense of hope while consolidating authoritarian control.

## Italy's Economic Struggles

Italy, though on the winning side of World War I, faced severe economic challenges, including high unemployment, strikes, and political unrest. Benito Mussolini's fascist movement leveraged these anxieties by portraying socialism and liberal democracy as threats to economic stability.

- **Suppression of Labor Movements**: Mussolini used the promise of law and order to suppress strikes and labor activism, framing his actions as necessary for restoring economic balance.
- **State-Led Recovery**: The regime implemented infrastructure projects and militarization, creating the illusion of economic progress while consolidating power.

---

## Modern Parallels: Economic Insecurity in the 21st Century

Economic anxiety remains a key driver of authoritarian and extremist movements in the modern era, often exacerbated by globalization, technological disruption, and financial crises.

## The 2008 Financial Crisis

The global recession that followed the 2008 financial crisis had far-reaching political implications, particularly in Europe and the United States:

- **Europe**: Economic austerity measures in countries like Greece, Spain, and Italy fueled populist and far-right movements. In Greece, the far-right Golden Dawn party capitalized on public anger toward immigration and the European Union, framing them as contributors to the crisis.
- **United States**: The loss of jobs and homes during the crisis led to widespread resentment toward elites and globalization. This resentment was later channeled into support for Donald Trump, whose rhetoric blamed immigrants, China, and international trade agreements for America's economic woes.

## Globalization and Job Displacement

The shift of manufacturing jobs to lower-cost labor markets has deepened economic insecurity in many developed nations. Populations in former industrial hubs, particularly in the U.S. Rust Belt, have experienced economic decline, fueling resentment:

- **Scapegoating Immigrants and Outsourcing**: Leaders and movements have framed immigrants and foreign labor as threats to domestic jobs, fostering anti-immigrant sentiment and protectionist policies.

- **Brexit**: In the United Kingdom, the Leave campaign exploited economic fears, portraying EU membership and immigration as detrimental to British workers and businesses.

## The Mechanics of Leveraging Economic Fear

1. **Identifying Scapegoats**: Economic fears are often directed toward marginalized groups, immigrants, or external actors (e.g., foreign nations or international institutions). This simplifies complex economic issues into a narrative of blame.
2. **Promising Simple Solutions**: Authoritarian leaders and movements present themselves as uniquely capable of solving economic crises, often through nationalist or protectionist policies.
3. **Amplifying Fear**: By emphasizing the consequences of inaction, such as job loss, cultural decline, or national collapse, leaders create a sense of urgency that overrides critical thinking.

## The Psychological Impact of Economic Insecurity

Economic anxiety triggers deep psychological responses that authoritarian leaders exploit:

- **Fear of Loss**: The fear of losing what one already has, whether a job, a home, or a way of life, creates fertile ground for radicalization.

- **Desire for Stability**: In times of uncertainty, individuals gravitate toward leaders and movements that promise order and security, even at the expense of freedom.
- **Us vs. Them Thinking**: Economic insecurity heightens tribalism, as people seek to protect their in-group from perceived threats posed by out-groups.

---

## The Consequences of Economic Exploitation

1. **Deepening Division**: Economic scapegoating fosters resentment and polarization, making constructive dialogue and solutions more difficult.
2. **Justifying Authoritarian Policies**: Measures framed as economic solutions—such as protectionism, immigration restrictions, or labor suppression—often serve to consolidate authoritarian power.
3. **Erosion of Trust in Institutions**: When economic fears are weaponized, trust in governments, financial systems, and international organizations declines, paving the way for populist uprisings.

---

## Lessons for Resilience

To counter the exploitation of economic anxiety, it is essential to:

1. **Address Root Causes**: Policies that reduce inequality, provide economic security, and support workers in

transitioning industries can alleviate the conditions that fuel extremism.

2. **Promote Economic Literacy**: Educating the public about the complexities of economic systems can reduce susceptibility to scapegoating and simplistic narratives.

3. **Build Social Cohesion**: Fostering unity and empathy across economic and cultural divides can weaken the appeal of divisive rhetoric.

---

Economic anxiety has always been a double-edged sword. While it can inspire collective action for positive change, it can also be manipulated to serve authoritarian agendas. By addressing the conditions that create economic insecurity and fostering resilience against fear-based narratives, societies can resist the pull of extremism.

In the next chapter, we will examine how cultural shifts and backlash against progress often intertwine with economic fears to create a fertile environment for authoritarian ideologies.

## Chapter 12: Cultural Shifts and Backlash

Cultural change is a double-edged sword. While progress toward equality, diversity, and inclusion is often celebrated as a sign of societal advancement, it also triggers backlash from those who see these shifts as threats to traditional values and power structures. Authoritarian rhetoric exploits this tension, framing cultural change as chaos and positioning itself as the guardian of "traditional" values. Throughout history, fascist movements have fixated on patriarchal and heteronormative structures, using them to justify exclusionary policies and consolidate power. The intersections of gender, sexuality, and race remain central to this strategy in both historical and contemporary contexts.

## Historical Fascist Obsession with Patriarchal and Heteronormative Structures

### Gender and the Idealized Family

Fascist ideologies have historically upheld rigid gender roles as the foundation of a stable society. The patriarchal family is portrayed as a microcosm of the nation, with the father as the authoritarian head, the mother as the nurturer, and the children as obedient citizens. This vision of the family becomes a template for governance, justifying the concentration of power in a single, unquestionable leader.

- **Nazi Germany**: The Nazi regime glorified women as mothers and caregivers, encouraging them to produce "racially pure" children to ensure the continuation of the Aryan race. Programs like the *Lebensborn* initiative provided incentives for women to bear children for the Reich, while those who stepped outside traditional roles faced discrimination or worse.
- **Mussolini's Italy**: Mussolini championed a vision of women as "reproducers of the nation," enacting policies to increase birth rates and discourage female participation in the workforce. The regime saw feminism and gender equality as threats to its patriarchal order.

## Sexuality as a Target

Fascist regimes also targeted LGBTQ+ individuals, portraying non-heteronormative relationships as deviant and corrosive to societal stability.

- **Nazi Persecution of LGBTQ+ People**: Under Hitler, homosexuality was criminalized, and gay men were sent to concentration camps. The regime framed LGBTQ+ people as enemies of the state, accusing them of undermining Germany's moral fabric.
- **Spain under Franco**: Francisco Franco's regime enforced strict moral codes rooted in Catholicism, targeting LGBTQ+ communities through censorship, imprisonment, and social ostracism.

## Race and Cultural Purity

Race was central to fascist ideology, with cultural and racial purity framed as essential to national strength.

- **Nazi Germany**: The Nazi fixation on Aryan supremacy justified the persecution of Jews, Romani people, and other marginalized groups. This obsession with racial purity extended to the arts, education, and media, with anything deemed "degenerate" banned or destroyed.
- **Italian Fascism**: Mussolini's embrace of racial laws later in his regime mirrored Nazi policies, targeting Jewish communities and reinforcing Italian imperial ambitions with rhetoric about racial superiority.

# Modern Parallels: Cultural Backlash in the 21st Century

## The Role of Gender and Sexuality

Cultural backlash in modern authoritarian rhetoric often centers on gender roles and LGBTQ+ rights, framing progress as an attack on traditional values.

- **Anti-Feminist Rhetoric**: Feminism is frequently portrayed as a threat to the family structure and societal stability. Leaders and movements emphasize a return to "traditional" gender roles, marginalizing women who seek equality or independence.
    - **Examples**: In countries like Poland and Hungary, governments have rolled back reproductive rights and restricted funding for gender studies programs, framing these actions as a defense of national values.
- **Targeting LGBTQ+ Communities**: LGBTQ+ rights are similarly framed as threats to morality, family, and religious freedom.
    - **United States**: Recent debates over transgender rights, drag performances, and gender-affirming care have been weaponized to stoke cultural division, with laws passed in several states to restrict LGBTQ+ expression.
    - **Russia**: Vladimir Putin's regime has passed laws banning LGBTQ+ "propaganda," positioning the state as the protector of traditional values against Western liberalism.

## Race and Immigration

Race continues to play a central role in modern authoritarian rhetoric, with immigration often framed as an existential threat to cultural identity.

- **Anti-Immigration Policies**: Leaders use fear of demographic change to justify restrictive immigration policies and xenophobic rhetoric.
  - **United States**: The rhetoric of building a border wall and restricting asylum has been paired with claims that immigrants threaten American jobs, safety, and culture.
  - **Europe**: Far-right parties across Europe have risen to prominence by framing Muslim immigrants as incompatible with Western values, fueling policies that marginalize minority communities.
- **The "Great Replacement" Theory**: This conspiracy theory, which falsely claims that white populations are being deliberately replaced by non-white immigrants, has gained traction in far-right circles. It mirrors historical fascist fears of racial and cultural dilution.

---

**The Backlash to Progress**

Cultural shifts toward equality and inclusion often provoke backlash because they challenge entrenched power structures. Authoritarian leaders exploit this fear of change to galvanize support, presenting themselves as defenders of tradition.

1. **Fear of Loss**: The perceived loss of cultural, gender, or racial dominance creates anxiety among privileged groups, making them receptive to divisive rhetoric.
2. **Simplified Narratives**: Complex societal changes are reduced to binary struggles—good versus evil, tradition versus modernity—fueling polarization.
3. **Moral Panic**: Leaders manufacture crises around gender, sexuality, or race to rally their base, positioning themselves as moral crusaders.

## The Consequences of Cultural Backlash

1. **Polarization and Division**: Cultural backlash deepens societal divides, creating an "us versus them" dynamic that undermines unity.
2. **Erosion of Rights**: Progress toward equality can be reversed as authoritarian leaders enact policies to suppress marginalized groups.
3. **Normalization of Oppression**: The framing of equality as a threat normalizes discriminatory practices, making them more difficult to challenge.

## Lessons for Resistance

To counter the authoritarian exploitation of cultural backlash, societies must:

1. **Defend Progress**: Vigilantly protect the rights and freedoms of marginalized groups, ensuring that cultural gains are not rolled back.
2. **Foster Empathy**: Promote understanding and dialogue across cultural divides to reduce fear and resentment.
3. **Challenge Rhetoric**: Expose the false narratives and moral panics used to justify exclusion and oppression.

---

Cultural shifts toward inclusion and equality are a sign of progress, but they also provoke backlash that can be weaponized by authoritarian movements. Recognizing and resisting these tactics is essential to preserving the hard-won advances that make societies more equitable and just. In the next chapter, we will examine the role of economic inequality and its relationship to the rise of authoritarian ideologies.

## Chapter 13: The Erosion of Truth

Truth is the foundation of democracy. When a society can no longer agree on basic facts, its ability to function as a collective deteriorates. Fascist movements have long understood this, using propaganda, misinformation, and conspiracy theories to undermine truth and sow confusion. In the modern post-truth era, the erosion of truth has reached new heights, fueled by digital platforms and the weaponization of disinformation. By examining how fascist politics has historically manipulated reality, and its modern parallels, we can uncover the dangers of living in a world where truth becomes a casualty.

---

## Historical Fascist Manipulation of Truth

### The Nazi "Big Lie" Strategy

Adolf Hitler's infamous concept of the "Big Lie" was predicated on the belief that people are more likely to believe an enormous falsehood than a small one, especially when it is repeated incessantly. Nazi propaganda used this tactic to:

- Blame Jews for Germany's economic and social woes.
- Convince the public that Germany was betrayed by internal enemies during World War I.
- Frame territorial expansion and war as acts of self-defense.

Joseph Goebbels, the Nazi Minister of Propaganda, refined this strategy, stating, "If you tell a lie big enough and keep repeating it, people will eventually come to believe it." The Nazis systematically erased inconvenient truths, replacing them with narratives that served their agenda.

### Fascism's Cultivation of Unreality

Fascist regimes often created a parallel reality where dissenting voices were silenced, and the state's narrative was the only acceptable version of events:

- **Italy under Mussolini**: Fascist Italy rewrote history textbooks, glorifying Mussolini as a national savior and emphasizing the superiority of Italian culture.
- **Franco's Spain**: Francisco Franco's regime suppressed alternative perspectives by controlling the press, censoring intellectual discourse, and punishing dissent.

By monopolizing truth, fascist leaders eliminated space for debate, ensuring that their version of reality was unquestioned.

---

## Modern Parallels: The Post-Truth Era

### The Rise of Conspiracy Theories

In today's political landscape, conspiracy theories have become a powerful tool for undermining truth and delegitimizing opposition:

- **QAnon**: This sprawling conspiracy theory has accused political and cultural elites of running a global cabal of child traffickers, using baseless claims to erode trust in democratic institutions.
- **Election Fraud Claims**: False allegations of widespread voter fraud in the 2020 U.S. presidential election led to the January 6, 2021, Capitol attack, highlighting how conspiracy theories can incite real-world violence.

### The Role of Social Media

Unlike in the 20th century, where propaganda was disseminated through state-controlled media, today's disinformation spreads through decentralized platforms:

- **Algorithms and Echo Chambers**: Social media algorithms prioritize sensational and polarizing content, creating echo chambers where users are exposed only to information that reinforces their existing beliefs.
- **Deepfakes and Misinformation**: Advances in technology, such as deepfake videos and AI-generated content, blur the line between truth and fabrication, making it increasingly difficult to discern reality.

**Erosion of Trust in Institutions**

The post-truth era has seen deliberate efforts to undermine trust in institutions that traditionally served as arbiters of truth:

- **Attacks on the Media**: Labeling the press as "fake news" delegitimizes investigative journalism and shifts attention away from factual reporting.
- **Distrust of Experts**: Movements that frame scientists, academics, and other experts as elitist or out of touch erode the public's confidence in evidence-based knowledge.

**The Mechanics of Undermining Truth**

1. **Overwhelming with Falsehoods**: Authoritarian movements flood public discourse with misinformation,

making it difficult for individuals to distinguish fact from fiction.

2. **Creating Division**: By presenting competing narratives, they fracture societal consensus, leaving citizens divided and less capable of collective action.

3. **Weaponizing Doubt**: Even if individuals don't believe a specific falsehood, the sheer volume of disinformation creates an atmosphere of distrust, weakening confidence in democratic systems.

---

## Consequences of the Erosion of Truth

1. **Polarization**: When shared realities dissolve, people retreat into ideological silos, deepening societal divisions.

2. **Inaction and Apathy**: The constant bombardment of conflicting information can lead to a sense of hopelessness, where individuals disengage from civic responsibilities.

3. **Empowerment of Authoritarianism**: A society unable to agree on basic facts becomes easier to manipulate, as authoritarian leaders position themselves as the sole sources of truth.

---

## Historical Parallels and Modern Risks

### Unreality in Action

The systematic manipulation of truth in the fascist era mirrors today's disinformation campaigns. Just as Goebbels crafted Nazi narratives that reshaped public perception, modern leaders use digital platforms to achieve similar outcomes:

- **Russia's Information Warfare**: Russia's government employs troll farms and state-controlled media to spread disinformation globally, framing its actions—such as the annexation of Crimea—as defensive or necessary.
- **Populist Rhetoric in Democracies**: Leaders in democratic nations increasingly adopt tactics that dismiss inconvenient truths, replacing them with simplified or outright false narratives to consolidate power.

### Lessons for Resilience

To counter the erosion of truth, societies must take deliberate steps to rebuild trust and promote media literacy:

1. **Strengthen Institutions**: Support independent journalism, transparent governance, and credible fact-checking organizations to ensure accountability.
2. **Educate Citizens**: Foster critical thinking skills and media literacy to equip individuals to navigate the complexities of modern information ecosystems.

3. **Demand Accountability**: Hold leaders, platforms, and institutions accountable for spreading misinformation and undermining trust in democratic processes.

---

The erosion of truth is one of the most insidious threats to democracy, creating a fertile environment for authoritarianism to flourish. Recognizing the patterns and tactics used to manipulate reality is the first step toward restoring trust and protecting the integrity of democratic systems. In the next chapter, we will explore how authoritarian leaders use economic and cultural fears to create cycles of dependence and control, examining the interplay between fear, loyalty, and power.

## Chapter 14: Weaponizing Education and Intellectuals

Authoritarian movements have always viewed education and intellectual freedom as double-edged swords. On the one hand, an educated and critical-thinking populace poses a threat to authoritarian control. On the other, education can be shaped into a tool to disseminate propaganda, suppress dissent, and reinforce ideological conformity. Fascist regimes in the 20th century weaponized education by targeting intellectuals, censoring ideas, and indoctrinating youth. Today, attacks on academia and critical thinking echo these tactics, highlighting the ongoing battle over the control of knowledge and its role in shaping society.

---

## Historical Suppression of Intellectual Freedom

## Fascist Italy and Germany: The Cultivation of Conformity

Both Mussolini's Italy and Hitler's Germany sought to control education and intellectual discourse, recognizing the power of knowledge to shape societal norms and values.

- **Nazi Germany**:
    - **Book Burnings**: In 1933, the Nazi Party orchestrated mass book burnings across Germany, targeting works by Jewish authors, Marxists, and others deemed "un-German." These events symbolized the regime's rejection of intellectual diversity and its desire to reshape cultural identity.
    - **Control of Curriculum**: Nazi-controlled schools replaced critical inquiry with ideological indoctrination. History classes glorified Aryan supremacy, and biology courses promoted eugenics. Universities purged professors who failed to conform to Nazi ideology, eroding academic freedom.
- **Fascist Italy**:
    - Mussolini's regime mandated the teaching of fascist ideology in schools, glorifying the state and emphasizing loyalty to the leader. Teachers who resisted were dismissed, and students were

funneled into fascist youth organizations to ensure ideological alignment from an early age.

**Spain under Franco:**

Francisco Franco's regime targeted intellectuals, viewing them as a threat to the regime's narrative of national unity under Catholicism and traditional values. Censorship extended to literature, film, and academia, suppressing any ideas that challenged the state's authority.

---

**Modern Parallels: Contemporary Attacks on Academia**

**Politicizing Education**

In today's polarized political climate, education has become a battleground, with attempts to control curriculum and censor ideas that challenge dominant ideologies:

- **United States**:
    - **"Anti-CRT" Legislation**: Several U.S. states have passed laws banning the teaching of critical race theory (CRT) or restricting discussions of systemic racism and inequality. These efforts aim to reshape history education to align with nationalist narratives, framing diversity and inclusion initiatives as divisive or unpatriotic.
    - **Book Bans**: The banning of books addressing LGBTQ+ issues, racial justice, and progressive values has surged, echoing historical attempts to restrict intellectual freedom.

- **India**:
  - Under Prime Minister Narendra Modi, history textbooks have been revised to downplay the country's Muslim heritage and emphasize Hindu nationalism. Critics argue these changes erase India's diverse past to align with the ruling party's ideological goals.

## Undermining Universities and Intellectuals

Authoritarian-leaning governments often portray academia as elitist, disconnected, or hostile to national values:

- **Brazil under Bolsonaro**: Former President Jair Bolsonaro repeatedly attacked universities, accusing them of promoting leftist ideologies and undermining traditional values. Budget cuts and censorship of research became tools to weaken intellectual independence.
- **Hungary under Orbán**: Viktor Orbán's government has restricted academic freedom by passing laws targeting gender studies programs and transferring control of universities to foundations aligned with the ruling party.

## Global Trends in Censorship

Advances in digital technology have enabled new forms of intellectual suppression:

- **Internet Censorship**: Authoritarian regimes like China and Russia closely monitor and control online discourse, targeting academics and intellectuals who share dissenting views.

- **Social Media Harassment**: Scholars who challenge dominant narratives are increasingly subjected to online harassment, often orchestrated by state actors or ideologically motivated groups.

## The War on Critical Thinking

Critical thinking—the ability to question, analyze, and evaluate information—is a fundamental threat to authoritarian control. By undermining this skill, authoritarian leaders create a more pliable populace:

1. **Promoting Ideological Conformity**: Education systems that emphasize rote learning over inquiry reinforce obedience and discourage dissent.
2. **Framing Intellectuals as Enemies**: Portraying academics as elitist or out of touch delegitimizes their expertise and makes it easier to suppress their influence.
3. **Discrediting Facts and Evidence**: In the post-truth era, authoritarian leaders often equate critical thinking with disloyalty, encouraging citizens to accept state-approved narratives without question.

## Consequences of Weaponizing Education

1. **Erosion of Democratic Values**: Restricting intellectual freedom undermines the ability of citizens to engage in informed decision-making, weakening democratic systems.

2. **Suppression of Innovation**: Societies that stifle critical thinking and academic inquiry limit their capacity for innovation and progress.
3. **Entrenchment of Authoritarianism**: Controlling education and intellectual discourse solidifies power by eliminating challenges to the regime's narrative.

---

## Lessons for Resistance

To counter the weaponization of education and intellectuals, it is essential to:

1. **Defend Academic Freedom**: Support policies that protect universities and educators from political interference.
2. **Promote Critical Thinking**: Encourage curricula that prioritize critical analysis, media literacy, and open dialogue.
3. **Foster Intellectual Diversity**: Celebrate and amplify diverse perspectives to counteract efforts to homogenize knowledge and suppress dissent.

---

Education is one of the most powerful tools for shaping a society, which is why authoritarian movements work so hard to control it. Recognizing the patterns of suppression and censorship, both past and present, is critical to defending intellectual freedom and ensuring that education serves as a catalyst for empowerment rather than oppression.

In the next chapter, we will explore how authoritarian regimes exploit economic disparities to consolidate power, examining the interplay between economic inequality and authoritarian control.

## Part IV: Resistance and Prevention

## Chapter 15: Lessons from the Anti-Fascist Struggle

History offers valuable lessons in how to resist authoritarianism and fascist movements. From the courageous actions of resistance fighters during World War II to the organized efforts of modern antifascist movements, the strategies and tactics employed by those who stood against fascism can serve as a guide for contemporary resistance. By examining historical case studies and modern parallels, this chapter explores the tools, methods, and philosophies that have proven effective in countering fascism.

---

## Historical Resistance: Standing Against Fascism

## The European Resistance During World War II

Across Europe, ordinary citizens, partisans, and underground networks risked their lives to fight against Nazi and fascist regimes. Their efforts illustrate the power of collective action and the importance of standing firm against oppression.

- **The French Resistance**:
    - The French Resistance was a decentralized network of fighters, spies, and informants who used sabotage, intelligence gathering, and guerrilla tactics to disrupt Nazi operations.
    - Despite the risks, resistance members successfully sabotaged railways, relayed critical intelligence to Allied forces, and helped shelter Jews and other persecuted groups.
- **The White Rose in Nazi Germany**:
    - A small but impactful student group in Munich, the White Rose distributed anti-Nazi leaflets and called for civil disobedience against Hitler's regime.
    - Their nonviolent resistance emphasized the moral imperative to speak out, even in the face of overwhelming danger. Though they were

ultimately executed, their legacy endures as a symbol of courage.

- **Partisan Movements in Italy and Eastern Europe**:
    - In Italy, partisans waged guerrilla warfare against Mussolini's forces and German occupiers, disrupting supply lines and liberating towns.
    - In Eastern Europe, partisan groups, including Jewish fighters in ghettos and forests, resisted Nazi extermination efforts, providing some of the most remarkable examples of resilience.

## The Role of Allied Forces

The defeat of fascism in World War II would not have been possible without the concerted efforts of Allied nations. While resistance movements within occupied countries played a crucial role, the broader military, economic, and moral support from Allied forces was indispensable.

- **Coalition Building**: The collaboration between diverse nations and ideologies demonstrated the necessity of unity in the face of a common enemy.

## Modern Antifascist Movements

## Antifascism in the 21st Century

Today, antifascist movements operate globally to counter the resurgence of authoritarianism and far-right extremism. These movements often combine grassroots organizing with digital activism to combat hate speech, disinformation, and authoritarian policies.

- **Direct Action**:
  - Groups like *Antifa* focus on disrupting fascist organizing efforts, often through direct confrontation and public demonstrations.
  - While controversial, their tactics aim to prevent the normalization of hate groups and their activities.
- **Digital Resistance**:
  - Modern antifascist efforts leverage technology to expose and counteract far-right networks. Activists use social media to amplify marginalized voices, debunk conspiracy theories, and organize protests.
  - Hacktivist groups have targeted hate groups by exposing their members and disrupting their online infrastructure.
- **Institutional Advocacy**:
  - Organizations such as the Southern Poverty Law Center (SPLC) and Hope Not Hate track hate groups, educate the public, and advocate for policies that counter extremism.

---

**Key Lessons from the Anti-Fascist Struggle**

1. **The Power of Unity**:
   - Resistance movements thrive on solidarity. Diverse coalitions—spanning political, racial, and

cultural lines—are essential for challenging authoritarian power.

- o Example: During WWII, resistance groups often collaborated with unlikely allies, uniting communists, liberals, and conservatives against fascism.

2. **The Importance of Local Action**:
   - o Grassroots efforts, whether through underground networks or local protests, can disrupt fascist momentum and provide immediate relief to affected communities.
   - o Example: Sanctuary movements that shelter marginalized groups from persecution draw on the legacy of WWII networks that protected Jews.

3. **The Role of Communication**:
   - o Countering fascist propaganda requires clear, consistent messaging that promotes inclusion and counters disinformation.
   - o Example: Resistance publications like those of the White Rose used concise, powerful language to inspire action and expose lies.

4. **Nonviolent and Violent Resistance**:
   - o While nonviolent tactics are often preferred, history shows that violent resistance, such as sabotage and armed uprisings, has also been effective in disrupting fascist regimes.
   - o Example: Partisan fighters in Italy and Eastern Europe relied on guerrilla tactics to weaken fascist forces.

## Challenges and Controversies

1. **Balancing Tactics**:
   - Modern antifascist movements face criticism for their methods, with some arguing that direct confrontation can escalate tensions.
   - Historical parallel: Resistance movements were often criticized during their time for being disruptive, yet history vindicates their efforts.
2. **The Risk of Normalization**:
   - Allowing authoritarian rhetoric to proliferate unchecked risks normalizing fascist ideologies. Resistance must be proactive, not reactive.
3. **State Suppression**:
   - Just as fascist regimes targeted resistance groups, modern governments often surveil and suppress antifascist activists, branding them as extremists.

## Lessons for Today

To build effective resistance against contemporary authoritarianism, we must draw on the lessons of history while adapting to modern challenges:

- **Educate and Mobilize**: Public education campaigns about the dangers of fascism and the importance of democratic values are crucial for galvanizing support.
- **Protect Democratic Institutions**: Strengthening legal safeguards and independent oversight can prevent authoritarian encroachment.

- **Foster Inclusive Communities**: Building resilient, inclusive societies weakens the appeal of divisive rhetoric and creates a bulwark against extremism.

---

## Conclusion

The anti-fascist struggle, past and present, demonstrates the resilience of people committed to justice, equality, and freedom. By learning from the successes and failures of these movements, we can equip ourselves to face the authoritarian challenges of today.

In the next chapter, we will explore strategies for strengthening democratic institutions, focusing on how to safeguard systems from authoritarian erosion and ensure the longevity of democratic governance.

## Chapter 16: The Role of Civic Engagement

Civic engagement is the foundation of resilient democracies. When citizens actively participate in their communities and political systems, they create a powerful defense against authoritarianism. Grassroots activism, local organizing, and collective action can disrupt authoritarian encroachment and foster a culture of accountability. This chapter examines how civic engagement has historically countered authoritarianism and offers practical steps for modern citizen resistance.

# The Power of Grassroots Activism

## Historical Examples of Civic Engagement

Throughout history, grassroots activism has been a driving force for social and political change, demonstrating that collective action can challenge even the most entrenched systems of power.

- **The Civil Rights Movement in the United States**:
  - Grassroots efforts like voter registration drives, boycotts, and sit-ins played a central role in dismantling segregation and advancing racial equality. Leaders like Martin Luther King Jr. mobilized communities to challenge oppressive systems through nonviolent resistance.
  - The Montgomery Bus Boycott (1955–1956) showcased the power of sustained local action, with ordinary citizens refusing to use public transportation to protest segregation laws.
- **Solidarity Movement in Poland**:
  - In the 1980s, the Solidarity trade union emerged as a grassroots movement opposing communist rule in Poland. Workers, intellectuals, and activists united to demand political and economic reforms, ultimately contributing to the fall of the Soviet-backed regime.
  - The movement's success highlighted the importance of building coalitions across societal divides.

- **Anti-Apartheid Movement in South Africa**:
  - Local organizing, coupled with international solidarity, was instrumental in dismantling apartheid. Boycotts, strikes, and community mobilization forced the South African government to confront the demands of a united populace.

---

## Modern Civic Engagement Against Authoritarianism

## Grassroots Activism in the Digital Age

Technology has transformed how citizens organize and resist authoritarianism, enabling rapid communication, broad mobilization, and global solidarity.

- **Pro-Democracy Protests in Hong Kong**:
  - Protesters in Hong Kong used encrypted messaging apps and decentralized leadership to organize mass demonstrations against China's encroachment on their freedoms. The movement's adaptability and reliance on technology kept it resilient in the face of state suppression.
- **Black Lives Matter Movement**:
  - The Black Lives Matter (BLM) movement exemplifies how grassroots activism can challenge systemic injustice. Social media platforms amplified the voices of activists, drawing attention to police violence and systemic racism while mobilizing millions worldwide.

- **Climate Activism**:
  - ○ Grassroots movements like Fridays for Future and Extinction Rebellion have galvanized young people to demand urgent action on climate change. These movements demonstrate how civic engagement can address global challenges and hold governments accountable.

---

## Practical Steps for Citizen Resistance

### 1. Build Local Networks

Grassroots movements begin with strong local networks. Engage neighbors, colleagues, and community groups to create a foundation for collective action.

- **Example**: Start or join a local organization focused on voter registration, environmental advocacy, or community education.
- **Tools**: Use social media to connect with like-minded individuals and share resources.

### 2. Educate and Empower

Knowledge is a powerful tool against authoritarianism. Educating communities about their rights and the mechanisms of democracy can foster empowerment.

- **Example**: Host workshops on media literacy, civic rights, or organizing strategies to counter disinformation and build informed communities.

## 3. Organize Peaceful Protests

Peaceful demonstrations can draw attention to injustices and galvanize public support.

- **Example**: Plan rallies, sit-ins, or marches to protest discriminatory policies or authoritarian actions. Partner with local organizations to maximize impact.

## 4. Advocate for Policy Change

Engage with policymakers to demand reforms that strengthen democratic systems.

- **Example**: Write letters, sign petitions, or meet with elected officials to advocate for fair voting practices, independent judiciary systems, or anti-corruption measures.

## 5. Support Independent Media

A free press is essential for holding power to account. Support independent journalism through subscriptions, donations, and sharing credible news sources.

- **Example**: Amplify investigative reporting that exposes corruption or human rights abuses.

## 6. Leverage Technology

Digital tools can enhance organizing efforts and counter authoritarian narratives.

- **Example**: Use platforms like Signal or Slack to coordinate actions, and create infographics or videos to disseminate information effectively.

## 7. Cultivate Resilience

Sustained activism requires resilience. Foster a culture of mutual support and prioritize mental health within activist communities.

- **Example**: Establish peer support groups to address burnout and celebrate small victories to maintain momentum.

## The Role of Community in Resistance

### Fostering Solidarity

Civic engagement thrives in communities that value solidarity and inclusion. Building bridges across racial, economic, and ideological divides strengthens movements and ensures that resistance is representative of society's diversity.

### Empowering Marginalized Voices

Authoritarian regimes often target marginalized communities first. Ensuring that these voices are central to resistance efforts not only enhances inclusivity but also addresses the root causes of injustice.

## The Ripple Effect of Civic Action

Civic engagement doesn't just challenge authoritarianism—it strengthens democracy by:

1. **Promoting Accountability**: Active citizens hold leaders and institutions accountable, ensuring transparency and fairness.
2. **Fostering Participation**: Engaged communities encourage broader participation in political processes, from voting to public dialogue.
3. **Building Trust**: Grassroots efforts create networks of trust that counteract the isolation and division often sown by authoritarian regimes.

---

## Lessons for Building Resilient Communities

1. **Start Small**: Change begins at the local level. Focus on tangible actions that address immediate needs while building momentum for broader movements.
2. **Stay Adaptable**: Be flexible in tactics and strategies, adjusting to changing circumstances and evolving challenges.
3. **Emphasize Collaboration**: Work with other groups and movements to amplify impact and build lasting alliances.

---

Civic engagement is the cornerstone of resistance to authoritarianism. By empowering individuals and communities to take action, we can create a robust defense against oppression and lay the groundwork for a more just and equitable society. In the next chapter, we will explore how strengthening democratic institutions serves as a long-term strategy for preventing the rise of authoritarian movements.

# Chapter 17: Strengthening Democratic Institutions

Democratic institutions serve as the foundation of a free society. They ensure accountability, uphold the rule of law, and protect individual rights. Yet, authoritarian movements often target these institutions, eroding their independence and credibility to consolidate power. Strengthening democratic institutions is vital for preserving democracy in the face of rising authoritarianism. This chapter outlines practical recommendations for safeguarding the judiciary, press, and elections, as well as the importance of maintaining robust checks and balances.

## Protecting the Judiciary

An independent judiciary is essential for upholding justice and maintaining the balance of power. Authoritarian regimes often seek to undermine courts, turning them into tools of the ruling elite.

## Threats to Judicial Independence

- **Historical Examples**:
    - In Nazi Germany, the judiciary was co-opted to enforce Nazi ideology, legitimizing discriminatory laws and persecution.
    - In modern-day Poland, the government has implemented reforms allowing political leaders to appoint and dismiss judges, eroding judicial independence.
- **Contemporary Risks**:
    - Politicization of the judiciary undermines public trust, reducing courts' ability to act as impartial arbiters of justice.

## Recommendations:

1. **Transparent Appointments**:
    - Implement transparent processes for judicial appointments to ensure merit-based selection and reduce political interference.
    - Example: Independent judicial commissions that vet and recommend candidates.

2. **Safeguard Tenure**:
   - Protect judges from arbitrary dismissal or intimidation, ensuring they can rule impartially without fear of retaliation.
3. **Public Awareness**:
   - Educate citizens about the role of the judiciary and its importance in safeguarding democracy.

---

## Defending a Free Press

A free and independent press is the cornerstone of informed citizenship and accountability. Authoritarian regimes often target the media, branding it as an enemy, censoring dissent, or spreading disinformation through state-controlled outlets.

## Threats to Press Freedom

- **Historical Examples**:
  - In Mussolini's Italy, the state controlled newspapers and used them to glorify fascism while suppressing dissent.
  - In Francoist Spain, strict censorship ensured that only state-approved narratives reached the public.
- **Modern Parallels**:
  - Governments in Russia and Turkey have cracked down on independent journalism, imprisoning reporters and shutting down critical outlets.

## Recommendations:

1. **Support Independent Journalism**:
   - Provide funding and legal protections for independent media to counteract state-controlled narratives.
   - Example: Public interest journalism initiatives like ProPublica.
2. **Combat Disinformation**:
   - Establish fact-checking organizations to identify and debunk false information.
   - Example: Platforms like PolitiFact and Snopes play key roles in maintaining media integrity.
3. **Legislative Protections**:
   - Enact and enforce laws protecting press freedom and safeguarding journalists from harassment or violence.

---

## Ensuring Electoral Integrity

Free and fair elections are the bedrock of democracy. Authoritarian leaders often undermine electoral processes through voter suppression, gerrymandering, or outright fraud.

## Threats to Elections

- **Historical Examples**:
   - In Nazi Germany, elections were reduced to symbolic events, with opposition parties banned and results pre-determined.

- o In Zimbabwe under Robert Mugabe, elections were marred by violence, intimidation, and voter fraud.
- **Contemporary Risks**:
  - o Disinformation campaigns, voter suppression laws, and cyberattacks threaten electoral integrity in democracies worldwide.

## Recommendations:

1. **Strengthen Voting Access**:
   - o Implement measures like automatic voter registration, early voting, and mail-in ballots to ensure broad participation.
   - o Example: States in the U.S. with high voter turnout often have accessible voting systems.
2. **Secure Election Infrastructure**:
   - o Protect voting systems from cyberattacks and foreign interference through robust cybersecurity protocols.
3. **Combat Disinformation**:
   - o Launch public education campaigns to counter false narratives about election fraud and promote confidence in electoral processes.

---

## Maintaining Checks and Balances

Checks and balances ensure that no branch of government wields unchecked power. When these mechanisms are weakened, authoritarianism can flourish.

## Threats to Checks and Balances

- **Historical Examples**:
  - Hitler's Enabling Act (1933) effectively dismantled legislative oversight, giving the Nazi regime dictatorial powers.
  - In Venezuela, Nicolás Maduro's government undermined the National Assembly, consolidating executive power.
- **Modern Challenges**:
  - Executive overreach and legislative gridlock erode the balance of power in democracies.

## Recommendations:

1. **Strengthen Oversight**:
   - Empower independent bodies to investigate corruption and hold leaders accountable.
   - Example: Anti-corruption commissions in countries like South Korea have exposed abuses of power.
2. **Protect Legislative Independence**:
   - Ensure that legislatures have the resources and authority to act as effective checks on executive power.
3. **Encourage Bipartisanship**:
   - Foster cross-party collaboration to prevent partisan politics from undermining institutional effectiveness.

## Lessons for Preserving Democracy

1. **Educate and Engage**:
   - Public awareness is critical for defending democratic institutions. Citizens must understand their role in holding these systems accountable.
2. **Build Global Solidarity**:
   - Democracies can learn from each other by sharing strategies for protecting institutions and countering authoritarian threats.
3. **Stay Vigilant**:
   - Even strong democracies are vulnerable to authoritarianism. Continuous effort is required to safeguard institutions and prevent erosion.

---

## Conclusion

Strengthening democratic institutions is a long-term strategy for resisting authoritarianism. By protecting the judiciary, press, and elections, and ensuring robust checks and balances, societies can build resilience against authoritarian encroachment. In the next chapter, we will explore how to cultivate a culture of civic responsibility and democratic values, empowering individuals to take an active role in safeguarding their freedoms.

# Chapter 18: Combatting Propaganda and Disinformation

Propaganda and disinformation have evolved into potent weapons in modern information warfare. Authoritarian regimes and movements use these tactics to manipulate public opinion, erode trust in institutions, and undermine democratic systems. Combatting these forces requires a multifaceted approach that empowers individuals, strengthens institutions, and leverages technology to promote truth and transparency. This chapter explores strategies for identifying and countering disinformation while rebuilding trust in democratic institutions.

## The Anatomy of Modern Propaganda and Disinformation

### Defining Propaganda and Disinformation

- **Propaganda**: The systematic dissemination of information, often biased or misleading, to promote a particular political agenda or ideology.
- **Disinformation**: False or misleading information spread deliberately to deceive or mislead, often used to sow confusion or erode trust.

### Key Features of Modern Information Warfare

1. **Speed and Scale**: Social media platforms amplify disinformation, enabling false narratives to spread rapidly and reach global audiences.
2. **Polarization**: Disinformation exploits societal divides, reinforcing echo chambers and fostering distrust.
3. **Plausible Deniability**: State and non-state actors use proxies or anonymous accounts to obscure the origins of disinformation campaigns.

### Historical Lessons on Combating Propaganda

### WWII Allied Efforts

During World War II, Allied forces countered Nazi propaganda by:

- Broadcasting truthful, compelling narratives via radio programs like the BBC's *War Reporting Unit.*
- Distributing leaflets that debunked Nazi claims and provided accurate information to occupied territories.

## Cold War Strategies

The United States and its allies used initiatives like *Radio Free Europe* to combat Soviet propaganda, emphasizing transparency and factual reporting to counteract communist disinformation.

---

## Modern Challenges: Disinformation in the Digital Age

### The Role of Social Media

Social media platforms are breeding grounds for disinformation:

- **Echo Chambers**: Algorithms prioritize content that aligns with users' existing beliefs, reinforcing biases.
- **Bots and Troll Farms**: Automated accounts and coordinated efforts amplify false narratives, making them appear more credible.
- **Deepfakes and Manipulated Media**: Advances in technology enable the creation of hyper-realistic but false content, further blurring the line between fact and fiction.

## Examples of Disinformation Campaigns

- **2020 U.S. Election**: False claims of widespread voter fraud undermined public confidence in the electoral process, contributing to the January 6 Capitol attack.
- **COVID-19 Misinformation**: Disinformation about the pandemic sowed confusion, undermined public health efforts, and deepened political divides.

---

## Strategies for Combatting Propaganda and Disinformation

### 1. Strengthening Media Literacy

Educating individuals to critically evaluate information is one of the most effective defenses against disinformation.

- **Promote Critical Thinking**: Teach people to question sources, identify bias, and differentiate between credible and unreliable information.
- **Encourage Verification**: Emphasize the importance of cross-referencing information with trusted, independent sources.
- **Provide Tools**: Platforms like *MediaWise* and *FactCheck.org* offer resources to help individuals identify disinformation.

### 2. Leveraging Technology

Technology can be a powerful ally in the fight against disinformation.

- **AI-Powered Fact-Checking**: Develop and deploy algorithms to identify and flag false content in real time.
- **Bot Detection**: Use tools like *Botometer* to identify automated accounts spreading disinformation.
- **Deepfake Detection**: Invest in technologies that can recognize and expose manipulated media.

## 3. Supporting Independent Journalism

A free press is essential for countering propaganda and promoting transparency.

- **Invest in Investigative Reporting**: Support journalists who uncover disinformation campaigns and expose their origins.
- **Protect Press Freedom**: Advocate for laws that safeguard journalists from harassment, censorship, and violence.
- **Amplify Credible Voices**: Promote reliable news outlets and initiatives like *ProPublica* and *Reuters Fact Check*.

## 4. Regulating Social Media Platforms

Hold social media companies accountable for their role in spreading disinformation.

- **Transparency Requirements**: Mandate disclosure of algorithmic processes and content moderation policies.
- **Content Moderation**: Encourage platforms to actively monitor and remove harmful disinformation.
- **Policy Enforcement**: Implement penalties for platforms that fail to address disinformation effectively.

## 5. Building Trust in Institutions

Disinformation thrives when trust in institutions is low. Rebuilding this trust is crucial for combatting false narratives.

- **Foster Transparency**: Governments, media, and organizations must operate transparently to restore public confidence.
- **Engage Communities**: Institutions should actively involve citizens in decision-making processes to demonstrate accountability.
- **Combat Corruption**: Strengthening anti-corruption measures can reduce the credibility gap exploited by disinformation campaigns.

## 6. Encouraging International Collaboration

Disinformation is a global challenge requiring coordinated responses.

- **Global Coalitions**: Countries should share intelligence, strategies, and resources to combat cross-border disinformation campaigns.
- **Countering Authoritarian Narratives**: Democracies must collectively challenge state-sponsored propaganda from authoritarian regimes.

---

## Lessons for Rebuilding Trust

1. **Be Proactive**: Address disinformation campaigns early before they gain traction.

2. **Engage at the Community Level**: Partner with local organizations to combat disinformation in ways that resonate with diverse communities.

3. **Celebrate Successes**: Highlight examples of successful efforts to counter disinformation, inspiring further action.

---

## Conclusion

Propaganda and disinformation pose existential threats to democracy, but they can be countered through education, technology, and robust institutional responses. By fostering media literacy, supporting independent journalism, and holding social media platforms accountable, societies can resist the corrosive effects of false narratives. In the next chapter, we will explore how promoting a culture of inclusion and empathy can serve as a powerful antidote to the divisive tactics employed by authoritarian movements.

## Chapter 19: Bridging Divides

Polarization is one of the most significant challenges facing democracies today. When societies are fractured along political, cultural, or social lines, authoritarian movements thrive by exploiting these divisions. Reducing polarization and fostering unity are essential to building a resilient democratic society. This chapter explores the strategies for bridging divides and building coalitions across ideological and social boundaries, creating a foundation for collective action against authoritarian threats.

# The Impact of Polarization

## The Dangers of Division

Polarization undermines the ability of societies to address shared challenges and leaves them vulnerable to manipulation:

- **Weakened Democratic Norms**: Extreme partisanship erodes trust in institutions, as citizens view opposing parties or ideologies as illegitimate.
- **Paralysis in Governance**: Divided societies struggle to enact policies that address systemic issues, deepening public disillusionment.
- **Fuel for Authoritarianism**: Leaders exploit division to consolidate power, framing themselves as the only figures capable of restoring order.

## Historical Examples of Polarization Exploitation

- **Germany (Weimar Republic)**: The political fragmentation of the Weimar Republic allowed Adolf Hitler and the Nazi Party to present themselves as a unifying force, despite their divisive and destructive ideology.
- **United States (Civil Rights Era)**: Resistance to civil rights reforms in the 1960s revealed deep societal divisions, which were exploited by politicians using dog-whistle rhetoric to maintain the status quo.

## Strategies for Reducing Polarization

### 1. Encouraging Civil Discourse

Open, respectful dialogue is a cornerstone of bridging divides. Creating spaces where individuals can share perspectives fosters mutual understanding.

- **Community Dialogues**: Programs like *Braver Angels* in the United States bring individuals from across the political spectrum together to discuss contentious issues in a constructive manner.
- **Active Listening**: Encouraging participants to listen to understand, rather than to respond, can reduce defensiveness and build empathy.

### 2. Promoting Shared Goals

Focusing on common values and objectives helps transcend ideological differences:

- **Historical Example**: During World War II, the Allied powers united despite differing political systems and ideologies to confront the shared threat of fascism.
- **Modern Application**: Local initiatives addressing universal concerns like education, healthcare, and community safety can bridge partisan divides by emphasizing shared interests.

## 3. Building Inclusive Coalitions

Effective resistance to authoritarianism requires diverse coalitions that bring together individuals and groups from various backgrounds:

- **Intersectionality**: Recognize that issues such as race, gender, and class intersect, and address these complexities to create more inclusive movements.
- **Coalition Examples**:
    - The *Women's March* brought together diverse communities to advocate for gender equality and social justice.
    - The *Poor People's Campaign*, inspired by Martin Luther King Jr., focuses on uniting individuals across racial and economic divides.

## 4. Combating Echo Chambers

Social media and digital platforms often reinforce polarization by exposing users to content that aligns with their existing beliefs. Breaking out of these echo chambers is crucial:

- **Algorithm Accountability**: Advocate for transparency in how platforms curate content, and push for measures to reduce polarization.
- **Promoting Diverse Perspectives**: Encourage media literacy and the consumption of information from a variety of reputable sources.

## 5. Addressing Root Causes

Polarization often stems from underlying grievances such as economic inequality, cultural insecurity, or systemic injustice. Addressing these root causes can alleviate tensions:

- **Economic Inequality**: Implement policies that reduce disparities and provide opportunities for marginalized communities.
- **Cultural Insecurity**: Promote initiatives that celebrate diversity while acknowledging the importance of cultural heritage.

---

## Building Trust Across Divides

### Trust as a Foundational Element

Trust is the glue that holds societies together. Rebuilding trust requires consistent effort and transparency:

- **Transparency in Governance**: Open government practices and clear communication foster public confidence.
- **Community-Based Solutions**: Engaging local leaders and organizations in decision-making processes ensures that diverse voices are heard.

### Overcoming Stereotypes

Authoritarian rhetoric often relies on stereotypes to deepen divides. Countering these narratives is essential:

- **Humanizing Opponents**: Share stories that highlight the humanity and complexity of individuals across divides.
- **Education Campaigns**: Promote programs that challenge stereotypes and encourage critical thinking.

## The Ripple Effect of Unity

Reducing polarization has far-reaching benefits for democracy and society:

- **Strengthened Institutions**: Unified societies are better equipped to defend democratic institutions and resist authoritarian encroachments.
- **Enhanced Problem-Solving**: Collaborative efforts lead to innovative solutions for complex challenges.
- **Resilience Against Manipulation**: Societies that value empathy and inclusion are less vulnerable to divisive rhetoric.

## Lessons for Building Bridges

1. **Start Small**: Focus on local initiatives where tangible progress can demonstrate the value of collaboration.
2. **Celebrate Success**: Highlight examples of cross-partisan achievements to inspire further efforts.
3. **Lead with Empathy**: Approach disagreements with a willingness to understand and find common ground.

Bridging divides is not about erasing differences but about fostering a culture where diverse perspectives can coexist and contribute to shared goals. By reducing polarization and building coalitions across social and political lines, societies can create a stronger, more unified front against authoritarianism. In the final chapter, we will explore how vigilance and active participation are essential for sustaining democracy and preventing the resurgence of authoritarian threats.

## Conclusion: A Call to Vigilance

## Chapter 20: Safeguarding Democracy for the Future

Democracy is not self-sustaining; it requires active participation, resilience, and an unwavering commitment to its core values. History has shown that authoritarianism does not emerge overnight—it grows in the cracks of weakened institutions, societal division, and unchecked power. Recognizing the warning signs and taking collective responsibility to prevent the rise of authoritarianism is essential for safeguarding democracy for future generations.

---

## The Lessons of History

## Recognizing the Warning Signs

The past offers a stark reminder of how authoritarian regimes rise by exploiting fear, economic instability, and social divisions:

- **Incremental Erosion**: Authoritarianism often takes root gradually, through small but significant attacks on institutions, civil liberties, and norms.
    - Example: Adolf Hitler's consolidation of power in the 1930s was achieved through legal means, exploiting societal divisions and crises.
- **Weaponized Polarization**: Divisive rhetoric and the framing of certain groups as enemies undermine national unity.
    - Example: The scapegoating of Jews in Nazi Germany created a pretext for mass persecution.

## The Cost of Complacency

When citizens disengage, the safeguards of democracy falter:

- **Historical Case**: The failure of the Weimar Republic to unify against the Nazi threat was exacerbated by political apathy and fragmentation.

- **Modern Parallels**: Declining voter turnout and disillusionment with democratic institutions leave societies vulnerable to manipulation and authoritarian encroachment.

---

## The Imperative of Collective Responsibility

## Why Democracy Requires Engagement

Democracy thrives when citizens actively participate in its processes. This includes not only voting but also engaging in civic life, advocating for transparency, and holding leaders accountable:

- **Civic Responsibility**: Apathy allows authoritarianism to grow unchecked. Active engagement strengthens institutions and ensures they serve the people.

## Rebuilding Trust in Institutions

Rebuilding trust is key to defending democracy:

- **Transparency and Accountability**: Governments must operate openly and be held accountable for their actions.
- **Community Involvement**: Local initiatives that empower communities to take ownership of democratic processes foster stronger connections between citizens and institutions.

## The Role of Education

Education is a cornerstone of democratic resilience:

- **Promoting Media Literacy**: Teaching citizens how to critically evaluate information reduces the effectiveness of propaganda and disinformation.
- **Understanding History**: Learning from the past equips citizens to recognize the early signs of authoritarianism and resist its encroachments.

---

## A Call to Action

### 1. Recognize Your Role

Every individual has a part to play in safeguarding democracy. This includes staying informed, participating in civic life, and standing against injustice:

- **Get Involved Locally**: Join community groups, volunteer, or run for local office to make a tangible impact.
- **Advocate for Inclusion**: Support policies and initiatives that promote equity and justice for marginalized groups.

### 2. Speak Out Against Injustice

Silence enables authoritarianism. Speaking out against divisive rhetoric, discriminatory policies, and attacks on institutions is essential:

- **Amplify Marginalized Voices**: Use platforms to uplift those who are disproportionately affected by authoritarian actions.

- **Challenge Falsehoods**: Confront disinformation with facts, promoting truth in both private and public discourse.

## 3. Build Coalitions

Unity is the antidote to division. Building coalitions across political, social, and cultural divides strengthens democracy:

- **Cross-Partisan Collaboration**: Work with individuals and groups from diverse backgrounds to address shared challenges.
- **Global Solidarity**: Join efforts to protect democratic values worldwide, recognizing that the fight for democracy is interconnected.

## 4. Stay Vigilant

Democracy's enemies often exploit complacency. Remaining alert to the warning signs of authoritarianism ensures early intervention:

- **Monitor Power Dynamics**: Watch for attempts to centralize power or weaken checks and balances.
- **Protect Civil Liberties**: Advocate for the preservation of free speech, press, and assembly, even when they challenge your own beliefs.

---

## A Vision for the Future

Safeguarding democracy is not a one-time effort but an ongoing commitment. By learning from history, fostering unity, and embracing collective responsibility, we can build a resilient society that defends its values against the threats of authoritarianism. This requires vigilance, courage, and an unrelenting belief in the principles of equality, justice, and freedom.

**For the Next Generation**

Democracy is a legacy we leave to future generations. By acting now, we ensure that our children and grandchildren inherit a world where their voices matter, their rights are protected, and their dreams can flourish.

---

**Closing Statement**

This book is both a reflection on the lessons of history and a guide for the future. The fight for democracy is a shared endeavor, one that demands the courage to stand against authoritarianism and the vision to build a world rooted in justice and equality. Together, we can ensure that the specter of fascism is relegated to the pages of history, never to rise again.

---

The call to vigilance is now in your hands. What will you do to safeguard democracy for the future?

# NOTES

# ABOUT THE AUTHOR

Pete Cossaboon is an angelic metaphysician who believes that we are spiritual beings first and foremost. With a deep understanding of the law of attraction, Pete encourages people to recognize their own power and potential to create the lives they truly want. He teaches that by aligning our thoughts, feelings, and actions with our deepest desires, we can manifest abundance, joy, and fulfillment in all areas of our lives.

Despite his profound spiritual insights, Pete has not been immune to the challenges of life. Like many people, he has struggled with depression at times, particularly as he has grown and moved through life. However, rather than letting his depression define him, Pete has used his spiritual wisdom and inner strength to overcome his challenges and embrace the path towards happiness and fulfillment.

Through his compassionate and insightful approach, Pete inspires others to recognize their own power and potential to overcome their own challenges and embrace the path towards happiness and fulfillment. He believes that by staying committed to our spiritual journey, and seeking out new avenues for growth and self-discovery, we can create lives that are aligned with our deepest values and aspirations. Whether we are struggling with depression or other challenges, Pete encourages us to remember that we are spiritual beings, capable of overcoming any obstacle that comes our way.

To work with Pete or to see more of his content, please visit, Http://www.PeteCossaboon.com